A LIGHTHEARTED BOOK
OF COMMON ERRORS

Don Hoeferkamp

Order this book online at www.trafford.com
or email orders@trafford.com

Most Trafford titles are also available at major online book retailers.

Printed in the United States of America.

ISBN: 978-1-4269-5426-9 (sc)
ISBN: 978-1-4269-5427-6 (e)

Library of Congress Control Number: 2011900667

Trafford rev. 01/31/2011

North America & international
toll-free: 1 888 232 4444 (USA & Canada)
phone: 250 383 6864 ✦ fax: 812 355 4082

To my four sons—Philip, Michael, Douglas, and Gary—in whom I'll
live after my earthly days are over

And to my four grandchildren—Courtney, Shelby, Natalie, and
Luke—the apples of their grandfather's eye

Foreword

I hope it's not **forward** of me to assert that you, gentle reader, are in for a real treat as you peruse the pages of this little volume, written by my colleague, mentor, and friend, Don Hoeferkamp.

I've known Don and admired his work for over 35 years. He's taught me so much about the English language and editorial precision. No one knows the language and its usage better than he. Even better, time after time I've laughed until my sides ached at his wry humor. It's true: Don never met a split infinitive he couldn't fix or a pun he didn't like!

Good for him! And it's good for us, too, because we all would be the happier for seeing life's quirks, absurdities, and challenges as Don does—with a smile on our hearts.

I commend this delightful treasure of wit and wisdom to you now. Savor and enjoy! You're not likely to turn any page without a grin lighting up your face (or a groan crossing your lips).

Dr. Jane L. Fryar
Writer/Editor

Epigraph

Whatever you are—be a good one.
-Abraham Lincoln

Acknowledgments

Since this is my first book, I'm unsure of how this section should go. I'll start by crediting my son Gary with planting the idea in my mind of originating a literary work. He announced that he himself was thinking of developing a book, and I considered that a goal to emulate.

I'm also very grateful to Doug, another son, for volunteering to transpose my handwritten text into the computer format desired by the publisher. He has done an outstanding job. Thanks go also to my sons Phil and Mike for their interest and encouragement along the way. I regard these four "shining stars" as very high among my many blessings!

Two other persons contributed their talents to this enterprise. Both are former employees of Concordia Publishing House in St. Louis, MO, where I also served for most of my editing career. The illustrator is Ed Koehler, an award-winning artist who lives and works in St. Louis. The author of the Foreword is Jane Fryar, a writer and editor in her own right, who now produces freelance materials from her home in Pacific, MO.

The three of us (Ed, Jane, and I) could be called (in the ancient Roman tradition) a triumvirate, except that Jane is not a *vir*, Latin for "man." However, she is full of **vim** and vigor in many ways, having published a number of successful books, many popular Bible studies, and hundreds of curricular lessons, primarily for children.

Finally, I would be remiss if I failed to acknowledge two persons who played a major role in my formation as an editor. My high-school Latin teacher in Columbus, IN, was George Utterback, who guided me to two state championships in Latin contests held in Bloomington, IN, which is the current location of Trafford Publishing®. And the man who interceded for me when I was hired at Concordia, and who gave me invaluable, hands-on training in the art of literary pursuits, is Dr. Allan Hart Jahsmann, of Los Angeles, CA. My mentor and dear friend is **still** writing books in retirement at the age of 94!

Introduction

"Just a spoonful of sugar helps the medicine go down." This alluring advice from a popular song captures what this book is about. Ordinarily, a book that deals with errors in grammar and word usage may seem like ill-tasting medicine in liquid form. We know that medicine is good for us and can help cure what ails us (without the **ale**), but we usually dislike the distasteful process of swallowing it.

*However, a spoonful of sugar **sweetens** the taste and helps the medicine go down "in the most delightful way." Likewise, a **lighthearted**, alluring approach to the vagaries of English usage and **mis**usage can make the process of assimilation sweeter and more delectable. It can transform mistakes into "a **comedy** of errors." "Lighthearted" means "happy, amusing, humorous, entertaining." **A Lighthearted Book of Common Errors** is designed to be all of these—with a big smile!*

"A cheerful heart is good medicine," a wise man once prescribed (Proverbs 17:22). No doubt most doctors today would concur. So following the "prescriptions" herein contained can result in making progress in language ability and thus gaining a cheerful heart. **That** could even help everyone save on medical expenses!

*Another long-standing proverb goes: "To err is human; to forgive, divine." Since all of us are human, we very likely err quite a bit. But I hope you will be divine enough to forgive me for calling attention to errors that you may at times incur, or that occur frequently in occurrences you, er, would just as soon "ferget." The fact that we all make errors doesn't mean that we are bad **persons**, however. We're still very valuable to the people around us, in whatever position in life we may occupy. But recognizing our mistakes and striving to overcome them can contribute to a **better** and **happier** life—and who doesn't want that?*

Sometimes it gets frustrating to experience a blizzard of common errors over the radio, on TV, and in books and magazines. (I'm not even going into the "personal" areas of e-mail, texting, tweeting, etc.) The snowdrifts expand into an avalanche as people pile up blunders parroted from others. There seems to be no end to such expressions as "each and every," "myself included," "try and go," "like I said," "lay down in bed," and countless others. What's a father to do?

*Of course, it's dreaming an impossible dream to try to reeducate the whole populace! We live in an imperfect world, and it will always be so. But can we at least make the effort to **improve** the way we speak and write? The world would be much lovelier if we didn't have to grimace at the (sometimes thoughtless) bungles that invade our space. (If you're blithely unaware of the existence of linguistic errors, you probably wouldn't be reading this. Congratulations that you are this far into the text! Felicidades!)*

So, as a father and grandfather, I decided the least I could do was to sensitize my own children and grandchildren to some areas in which they can **excel**, and thus help in a small way to upgrade the general level of competence in English. If anyone else can profit from the pointed pointers in this publication (that's also my hope), so much the better. So if I appear to be tilting at windmills in this endeavor, at least I'm on the same quixotic quest as **another** Don, who became quite famous as a result!

The revelations in this thin volume should be valuable to many kinds of seekers and searchers: teachers, students, journalists, broadcasters, authors, editors, librarians, public-relations and *human-resources personnel, advertisers, business leaders, lawyers, professors, pastors, priests, rabbis, playwrights, actors, politicians on every level, and all others who are interested in words, humor, and pleasurable reading. The catchiness of puns and other wordplays is intended to **lure** you back time and again to parts of the text that intrigue you, and thus fasten certain certainties more firmly in your memory and eventually into your mode of thinking and communicating.*

If you "digest" the clarifications made in the book—and review them at times—you'll find yourself **noticing** when common mistakes happen repeatedly. In fact, the goofs will start to **pop out** at you! And you'll be able to tell yourself, "I know better than that. Maybe I don't need to swallow everything I hear and see."

*By no means do these 100 common errors exhaust the list. But if you master many or most of the "top 100," you will have taken a giant stride toward becoming a better-informed person. And who knows? Maybe you'll start adding other common flubs that **you** discover (when you get in the habit of noticing them). Eventually, perhaps, our whole society will have taken a "**giant leap**" toward more mature writing and speaking!*

One more value of this collection is that it gathers **into one place** many errors that are commonly described or **pro**scribed, but that would be hard to find in a single location. Some of the entries may make your head spin, but that's part of the fun. In the spirit of Dr. Seuss, some items are spoofs and others are quite direct. I'll let you decide which category applies in each case. **All** have a serious **purpose**, though, and that's another discovery for you to realize.

*So, as Dr. Seuss might have put it, **let's get on with it!** And don't be afraid to laugh till it hurts. (There's a spoonful of sugar to take care of that too!)*

Contents

Absence of Other and Else

Today's mail brought this interesting statement for me to sign: "Like so many citizens, I am inspired to help the people of poor nations." Hold on a minute! Where are your manners? Although I certainly agree that we need to help poverty-stricken people, I'm insulted that I'm not considered a full-fledged citizen!

Why am I upset? It's because the proposed statement **excludes** me from the group referred to as "citizens." I'm **like** them, but in reality that means I'm **outside** them. The problem is that the little word "other" is missing. Add "other" to that group of citizens, and I become **one of** them. I'm like many **other** people; therefore, I'm part and parcel of that constituency. Thank you very much!

A similar gaffe occurs when the word "else" is absent (without leave) from a statement of comparison. Consider this opinion garnered from a news broadcast: "He did more than anyone to bring back the economy." Do you realize what that means? It means "he" (whoever it was) did more than **he himself** did! "He" is definitely part of the group called "anyone," isn't "he"? Definitely! So it's ridiculous to maintain that "he" did more than **anyone**. He couldn't outdo himself! But if "he" had been credited with doing more than anyone **else**, that's at least believable.

Absent "other" and "else," we're often left high and dry. But with these crucial words added, we're left low and wet—no, I mean we're home free! (Tennis, anyone **else**?)

Absolutely/Exactly

I'm absolutely certain that you will understand exactly what I'm getting at as I compose this page. There's absolutely no reason for you to feign ignorance of my point. In fact, it's exactly **for** this reason that I'm conceding that this item is absolutely unnecessary. (But it's here anyway.)

Where have all the "certainlies," "for sures," and "that's rights" gone? Gone to "absolutely" and "exactly"—every one! Why don't we simply excise ordinary declarations of certainty from our ordinary speech? After all, we have "exactly" and "absolutely." What further **need** have we of saying "that's right" or "certainly"—or just "yep"? (My granddaughter likes "yep." Maybe there's still hope for coming generations!)

I will also concede that no error is committed by the use of "absolutely" and "exactly." They are absolutely respectable verbal weapons to wield. But will you grant that it's possible to **over**stress and exaggerate by using these over-the-top expressions **ad nauseam** (look ahead to page 3)? We even have a word for exaggeration; it's called "hyperbole." (See Appendix 1 for the proper pronunciation of "hyperbole." It does **not** rhyme with "coal.")

Several decades ago the "in" word was "definitely." I **definitely** remember that. Now "definitely" has seemingly gone by the wayside. Will the same thing happen to "exactly" and "absolutely"? I absolutely hope so. That's exactly why "exactly" and "absolutely" rate an appearance in this book, though (as I said) they're totally unnecessary!

Ad Nauseum/Ad Nauseam

When someone says or writes "**ad nauseum**," I become nauseated! Why? Because they're trying to use a Latin phrase without knowing the correct pronunciation or spelling. They've probably **heard** the second word pronounced "nause**um**" and assumed that it must be spelled with an "um" at the end. But they've heard and spelled and pronounced incorrectly.

Another possibility is that someone who is writing a poem is trying to think of a word that rhymes with "mu**se**um." The only rhyming sound that comes to mind is "nau**se**um." But that may get the patron of the museum only as far as the restroom rather than a display room!

The correct Latin phrase is "ad nause**am**," meaning "to the point of nausea." So all you have to remember is to add a final "m" to the word "nausea"; then you'll be using both Latin and English in the right way (and helping me avoid that distasteful feeling of nausea).

Affect/Effect

These two words are very close in meaning (and spelling), so close that they're often confused or turned around. Someone may write or say, "I don't feel any **affects** of my illness." Surely the illness did affect the patient in some way, but there may have been no after**effects**. One little vowel ("a" or "e") can fell us if we aren't careful!

The definition of "af**fect**" is "to have an influence on," to "touch" or "move." "**Ef**fect" means "to bring about a result." So if a person is affected enough by an outside influence, it's likely to cause an effect on him or her. (Thus it's helpful to remember the phrase "cause an effect"—or is it "cause **and** effect"?)

In effect, we can effectively put to rest any misgivings about which word to se**lect**. We won't be affected negatively if we keep all our personal "effects" in the right place, especially if that place is a drawer, closet, or suitcase.

However, it seems that many persons today **skirt** the dilemma altogether by substituting "impact" for "affect." For them, everything gets impacted by an impact that is impactful. Perhaps the effect of the brainteaser on this page will be to impact their "**af**fects" (feelings) so much that they'll notice **no** ILL effects after the exercise—which would be known as **after**effects, if there were any!

Alumnus/Alumni

Sometimes it helps to know a little Latin. Evidently, one of the professors at a professional school that **requires students** to learn Latin didn't know much Latin himself. He wrote: "I am an **alumni**" (of a certain university).  Such a prominent gaffe could jar the bejabbers out of a person in the know. For in Latin, "alumn**i**" is the **plural** form of "alumn**us**." It's as if the professor had said, "I am a **people**"! (Now I'm wondering whether the other shoe will drop: someone exclaiming, "We are alumnuses!")

But there's another aspect to the Latin term for graduate or former student. Since Latin conveniently designates both gender and number by word endings, a woman in this context is called an "alumn**a**" and a number of women "alumn**ae**."

So we need to be very careful about how we refer to graduates or former students of a particular school. Maybe we should just shorten all the terms to the generic "alum" and "alums," thus avoiding possible predicaments like the ones mentioned. But would that be fair to the ancient Romans, who came up with such useful distinctions as "alumnus/a" and "alumni/ae"? Ah, for some illumination from you class **lumens** out there!

Amidst/Amongst/Whilst

(If you're a citizen of the United Kingdom, you may skip this page. Your cultural and linguistic heritage probably rules out its applicability to you. Of course, you're **welcome** to read it anyway, just for laughs!)

"**Whilst** I'm in the **midst** of joking **amongst** my friends, I get a lot of ang**st amidst** my laughter." Though this made-up quote is exaggerated, you'd be surprised how many people needlessly tack on "st" endings like these after common adverbs, nouns, and prepositions. Maybe they think they're being cool by using cute-sounding language. Perhaps they want others to think they're smart because they know alternative endings to common words. Or could they just want to **sound** elitist? (Poets, of course, can be given a pass.)

To the average person in the crowd, though, these "st" words sound a little **weird**, as if they're being resurrected from centuries long gone. If some speakers and writers persist in using them, why "don'tst" they go all the way and convert "when" to "whenst," "where" to "wherst," and "unknown" to "unbeknownst"? (Wait—they've **already** converted that last one!) We could even give them stilts to stand on so they wouldn't merely **sound** stilted!

Maybe if we complained enough, we could reverse the trend toward the use of obsolete terms. "Whilst" would revert to "while"; "amongst" would become the normal "among"; "amidst" would shorten to "amid"; and "midst" could return to "middle." Enough already with the "st's" in our midst!

Better/Best

Good, better, best—never let it rest
Till your good is better, and your better best!

There's something to be said for wanting to be better than good, and for trying to be the best instead of just better than the rest. So how do you rate yourself—good, better, or best?

When it comes to knowledge of grammar, you probably hope to be at least as good as, if not better than, the rest. That's one reason you're out to improve yourself by doing what you're doing now: reading, learning, and "inwardly digesting" tips that are helpful.

If you watched or read about some of the World Cup soccer games held in South Africa in 2010, you may recall what one coach deduced after his team lost to the eventual winner. His summary of the fierce action was: "They were the **best** team with the ball." We can allow for the fact that the coach wasn't quite up to **snuff** on his English, if indeed he spoke in English. But we can surely **sniff** out the error in the **stuff** that was said.

Okay; what **was** the error? Remember that only two teams were on the playing field. So how could one of them be the **best**, since "best" is the superlative degree of "good"? "Best" applies only when **more than two** are being compared; at least three have to be in the equation. "**Better**" applies when **two** things or persons are being compared: one is "better" than the other. So the coach should have said (if he spoke English, of course), "They were the **better** team with the ball."

I hope you're better prepared now to strive for the best in your native tongue (if English is indeed your native tongue). It's good to be **better**, but even better to be **best**!

Born/Borne

Getting "born" and "borne" mixed up is a common error. Let's see if we can get these twin terms straightened out.

Before you were **born**, you were **borne**—that is, carried by your mother. (Soon after birth you may have been borne, or carried, also in a baby carriage.) If you **hadn't** first  been borne, you would not have been born! (Aside: It's good to be **well**born, but even better to be well-**borne**. And if you were the **first**born child, you were also the first one borne.)

A **bare** little letter like an "e" can make quite a difference in meaning between two similar words, as we just saw. So it's good to watch your "p's," "q's," **and** "e's." If you do, you'll realize, for instance, that diseases born when water **carries** them are water-borne diseases!

Should we play a little more (or **barely** more?) with "born" and "borne"? An author could begin a novel with a catchy sentence like this: "I was born to be borne on a magic carpet and transported as a born-**again** person from the **Ber**ing Sea to **Mel**bourne, where dreams are born—almost like the magic dragon that lived by the sea and frolicked in Honah Lee!" (If you're in a creative writing class, try expanding on that bare opening.)

A much-loved hymn opens with "I was there to hear your borning cry." Bear with me now as we continue in this book to explore a number of "bornings" in the field of language—some carried out (or borne) in high style, and others, sadly, born out of inexperience or inattention.

It barely bears repeating that if you watch out for and avoid such common errors as the one detailed here, you may very well develop an **un**common **bearing** in your personal **carriage**!

Chaise Lounge/Chaise Longue

Would you like to know a term that practically **everybody** gets wrong? I myself was one of those "everybodies" until I accidentally stumbled upon the right spelling and pronunciation in a dictionary. (See what nice things dictionaries are to have around!)

What is this term? I'll give you a clue. It identifies something you lie on when you want to sun yourself in the backyard or on the beach. You actually **lounge** on this object. That's why almost everyone refers to it as a chaise **lounge**.

Look in ads and circulars from stores that sell these "loungy, couchy" things. Invariably, the ads contain the spelling "chaise lounge." But guess what? To correct the mistake, you have to switch several of the letters around so that you end up with (or fall flat on) "chaise **longue**."

The confusion arises because this is a **French** expression. Appropriately enough, it means "long chair." And get this: the second word is actually pronounced "LONG"! It's almost like "tongue," right? We don't, or shouldn't, pronounce the final "ue" in either word.

So if you want to relax and "clown around" for a while (see the book's cover), invest in a chaise **longue** and have a **long** nap, **chas**ing your dreams while you **lounge** in style!

P.S. "Chaise" is pronounced "SHAZ," not "CHAZE," another surprise. So while you're peacefully resting, practice saying "SHAZ LONG."

Come See/Come Try/Come Go

Laziness and sloppiness have a way of infecting our use of language without our being aware of what's going on. "Come see us," a pharmacy advertises in a huge headline. "Come try our service," other vendors plead. "Come go with me," runs a common invitation.

What these tempting appeals have in **common** is that they splice two verbs together, with nothing between them. Maybe this lazy practice has been practiced for a long time, but in **recent** times it has seemingly mushroomed

a thousandfold. Regrettably, though, it's a sloppy habit to combine two verbs without a connective, such as "and" or "or" or even a comma!

Someone may retort, "Go fly a kite!" But I'd prefer they would add a comma: "Go, fly a kite!" I really don't **have** a kite to fly, but I'd feel less offended if I were told **first** to go and **then** to fly (two actions, separated by a comma). Furthermore, "Come **and** go with me" would stand a much better chance of my accepting the invitation than it would without the "and." (Now you know how to please me, I hope.)

The Bible has it right (as usual) when in Mark 6:31 we are urged: "Come . . . apart . . . **and** rest awhile." Just be careful not to come **too far** apart!

Compliment/Complement

I was astounded, to say the least, when I encountered this boast on the menu at an upscale restaurant: "Our wine list **compliments** our cuisine"! That's about as far as a good wine list can go; to "compliment" the cuisine is a great compliment indeed! I wonder what words the wine list used in praise of that feast of food, which must have been extraordinary.

In the **ordinary** course of affairs, wine lists **complement** the cuisine—in other words, they fill it out or enhance it with extra flavor and zest. I guess that **could** be regarded as a special compliment, but only if the wines were capable of reason and purpose—a huge stretch!

A young pastor once asked how to keep the distinction clear between "compliment" and "complement." One way is to connect "complement" with the word "complete." When one person or thing **completes** another, the two can be considered **complementary**. They fulfill or enhance each other.

Take the example of an ideal husband and wife. They definitely complete **and** complement each other. But if one of these partners happens to partake too freely from a wine list, the other partner may offer the very opposite of compliments: **detrimental** remarks. And that could lead to a complete undoing of a complementary relationship!

Could (Couldn't) Care Less

Here's the way a prominent person in the news put this phrase: "I **could care less** about my legacy." Now, if this person **could** care less, why **doesn't** (s)he care less than at the present? That's a real puzzler!

The truth is, the person actually **does** care very little or not at all about leaving behind a legacy (a record of accomplishments or a gift to heirs). The person really **can't** care less than (s)he already does. Therefore, the speaker should have said, "I could **not** care less [than the little or none I care now] about my legacy."

Ergo: Use "couldn't care less" rather than carelessly using "could care less," un**less** you really **could** care less!

P.S. I (the author) couldn't care **more** (than I already do care) about your opinion of this book.

Dangling Participles

Would you buy insurance from a company whose ad stated: "Working toward your savings goals on a gradual basis, **it will be easier** to adjust to seeing less in your paycheck"? I certainly wouldn't! (Later in this book we'll see why the phrase "on a gradual basis" isn't so hot. "Gradually" is preferable.)

But for now, I'm completely turned off by the opening participle, "working." Why? Because it just hangs in thin air, ostensibly attached to "**it**." But "it" doesn't have any savings goals. It's just an it! Logically, "working" needs to be followed by "**you**," because **you're** the one who's working. Isn't that fairly obvious?

Lots of times people will start a sentence with an "ing" word (usually a participle or gerund) and then lose their train of thought. So they leave us **dangling** in a cloud of thick smoke. The **who** or **what** that the "ing" word is supposed to refer to doesn't get mentioned. What a crock!

A dangling participle without an appropriate noun or pronoun to modify is like a monkey trying to hang from a tree limb without a limb to hang onto. (In fact, "dangling" participles are also **called** "hanging" participles.) Maybe we should call the animal a "limbless monkey," a monkey without limbs. And if the monkey falls to the ground, it will probably need some of that "monkey-bottom powder" I've been seeing in stores!

So when you encounter an "ing" word at the start of a sentence, wait to find out if it dangles. If it does, hang it up!

Data Is/Data Are

Maybe you heard it on national TV, as I did. A very intelligent person gave this summary of the day's events: "We won't know more until additional **data is** in." Of course we need additional data before we can know more. But that isn't the point here. The point is that "data is" is wrong, at least in most circumstances. (Would anyone say, "Until additional **facts is in**"?)

"Data" is the **plural** form of the Latin word *datum*, which means factual information. (Notice that **that** "data is" is okay, because we're referring to "data" as a **single word**.) So when we speak of more than one factual detail, we need to use the plural word "data." And plural nouns take plural verbs, the last I heard. So "**data are**" is the correct form most of the time. (Sorry about that "are is," but it **is** right!) Is all this data confusing, or what? Or should that be "**Are** all **these** data confusing?" Now **I'm** confused!

Dates of the year are one kind of data. Also, dates between lovers could be very important data in their courtship. Maybe even dates that are

eaten would be data in one's diet plan. So data involve (not "involves") many dates and other details, but one thing data are **not** is "**is**"!

P.S. The preferred pronunciation of "data," in case you're wondering, is "DAY-tuh." At least we can agree on that, **can't we**?

"How do you like those data?"

Did You Know?/Do You Know?

Do you know that "**Did** you know?" may not be the preferable way to begin a question about someone's knowledge? I won't fault you for saying, "Did you know?"—because nearly everyone does it. I myself am guilty of this habit, if "guilty" is the right word.

But is it **logical** to use "did" rather than "**do**"? Think it through. "Did" is past tense, of course. So we're actually asking about someone's knowledge in the past or about the past, when we really want to know what they know **right now**! They may have known an answer or a fact before we asked the question, but do they **still** know it? Wouldn't it be more sensible to ask, "**Do** you know?"

You know what? It probably isn't going to make a huge difference whether we switch to "Do you know?" most of the time. It's very hard to break addictions and habits in the ways we employ language. But please **know** that it's **good** to know what the best choices are, even if we don't always follow them—no?

P.S. On the contrary, there's a saying from Jesus in the Bible (John 13:17) that goes: "If you **know** these things, happy are you if you **do** them"! (I know; I know; I'm quoting out of context. Isn't that okay if it suits your purpose??)

Different Than/Different From

How would it sound to hear or see a statement such as "This brand **differs** very little than that one"? Weird, right? So if we change the statement to one you're more likely to encounter—"This brand is very little **different than** that one"—why is it any better? (It isn't!)

When we use the word "different," we're setting **apart** two or more persons, places, or things. So it makes no sense to employ a **comparing** word ("than") to express the difference between or among different entities. "What's the difference between 'than' and '**from**'?" you may ask. Well, what's the difference between day and night?

Really, the word "from" is much clearer than "than" after "different." "From" in this case indicates a **separation**, which is what "different" connotes. So be different from the "different than" folks and go with "different from."

See how much better it sounds to hear: "This brand differs very little **from** that one"! If you beg to **differ**, well then, **be** different!

Each and Every

The phrase "each and every" has at least two strikes against it. One more, and it will have to head for the dugout!

First, "each and every" is a cliché—and clichés by their very nature are a turnoff, unless used for effect or in mockery. Apparently, some speakers and writers think of "each" and "every" as identical twins that can't be separated, and automatically join them at the hip, in Siamese fashion. It seems the word-makers can't even **conceive** of one without the other!

Second, the phrase is redundant, another gross-out. The words "each" and "every" **are** practically identical; they mean or imply much the same thing. So why do we have to listen to or read this pointless repetition so often? It gets to hang out, doesn't it? And well it **should** hang out—to dry!

"Each and every" time someone refers to "each and every time" you do something or go somewhere, you can almost guess they aren't using their brain. It's a no-brainer that in **your** brain (mind) they ought to dry **up**!

Each Other/One Another

It seems that many persons don't have a clue about the difference between "each other" and "one another." In fact, sometimes they interchange these two phrases in the same context, as if there **were** no difference at all. If there is no difference, why do we have **both** phrases in our language? Can't we just eject one of them to simplify matters?

I've heard sports announcers tell about two players "fighting **one another**." And the members of some families may boast of "how much we all love **each other**." So how do we distinguish between these two common expressions? What **is** the difference if we intend to retain them both?

A simple rule suffices: "Each other" should be used when we refer to **two** people; "one another" indicates that **more than two** are involved. "Love one another" is advice given to **all** members of a religious community. But if just two of them are together, they would be urged to "love **each other**."

Since we're all in this together, let's help one another out by supporting each other when we're in pairs, and by encouraging one another when we're all together. I hope you have all of this altogether absorbed, even when you happen to be **in** the altogether!

P.S. A similar situation exists between "between" and "among." "Between" links **two** entities or people. "Among" is the proper preposition when **more than two** are involved. "Between the four of us" would sound bizarre; "among you and me," likewise.

Eager/Anxious

I'm not too **eager** to write this. That's because I'm **anxious** about the reception it will have. However, some readers or viewers may think it's "much ado about nothing," as in the play by Wm. Shakespeare.

Allow me to rephrase the first two sentences: I'm not too **anxious** to write this. That's because I'm **eager** about the reception it will have. Do you catch the difference in meaning? It shouldn't be too hard to do, unless you're overly anxious about it.

This little exercise proves a point about "eager" and "anxious." "Eager" is a **positive** word. It suggests an urgent desire to do something uplifting or to engage in a worthy cause. "Anxious" is a **negative** word. It connotes unease and worry, bordering on fear, about an impending action or event.

Often, though, speakers and writers throw in an "anxious" when they mean to forecast a positive outcome, as in "I'm anxious to go on my vacation." If one is really **eager** to take a trip, why would one **worry** or harbor a **fearful** (anxious) attitude about it?

Now that I've overcome my **anxiety** about preparing this item, I'm **eager** to go on to the next one—eager as a beaver!

Eating Healthy/Healthily/Healthfully

How do you eat? I don't mean how you use your mouth or how you swallow. I mean in what **manner** you eat. That could encompass a lot of ways: heartily, slowly, gluttonously, or what have you.

Our concern here, though, concerns the contemporary focus on **healthy** eating. We're inundated with rigorous diet plans and organic food selections that attempt to make and keep us healthier. I'm not knocking this trend; I think it's wholesome and healthful.

Actually, our primary interest in the context of this book is the terminology we use with respect to eating, specifically the adverbs and adjectives that modify this activity. I see everything from "eating healthy" to "eating healthily" and "eating healthfully." (Care to guess which of these expressions we'll end up favoring?)

"We've all heard how important it is to eat **healthy**," ran a newspaper feature. What say you about **that** terminology? "Healthy" is an adjective, and adjectives don't like to modify verbs! "Healthy eating" is okay, because an adjective modifies a noun ("eating"). But we can eliminate "eating healthy." (To me, even "eating a healthy **diet**" sounds strange. We eat **food**, not diets.)

"Eat **healthily**" is somewhat better, because "healthily" is an adverb modifying a verb. But the phrase still doesn't ring true as a way to talk about eating. "Healthily" is just the adverbial form of "healthy," and we've already shown that that's an inferior descriptive for "eating."

This leaves us with "eat **healthfully**." Whereas the main emphasis of "healthy" is on **possessing** good health, the main emphasis of "healthfully" is on being **conducive** to good health. That's the way I like to eat, and I hope you like it too!

E.g. and I.e.

These initials or abbreviations are cute little ways of taking shortcuts. It's such a cool-sounding ploy to drop an "i.e." into one's oral or written comments. (This happens frequently on TV talk shows.) However, if "i.e." doesn't express what you mean to say, it turns out to be a downright embarrassment!

Here again, a knowledge of Latin comes to the rescue to help us decipher this code-language. "E.g." stands for *exempli gratia*, meaning "for (the sake of) example." The initials "i.e." stand for *id est*, meaning "that is"—namely, "**namely**."

It's more common for journalists and others to plug in an "i.e." when they should use an "e.g.," rather than the other way around. In other words, they are saying "that is" or "namely" when actually they are following up with one or more **examples**!

So whenever you hear (or see in print) someone citing an example or a string of examples after using an "**i.e.**," tell yourself: "**Eiyeee**—that's wrong! They really mean '**e.g.**' "

P.S. It's better not to use a foreign word or expression at all if you don't really know what it means.

Either Side/Both Sides

"Houston, we have a problem." It seems confusing that "either" can have two different and even contradictory meanings: (1) Being the one or the other of two; (2) Being the one **and** the other of two. I hesitate to disagree with the dictionary. After all, who knows how two such uses for the same word came to be? So if you want to say, write, or enter "on either side of the ocean" and mean **both** sides, you're welcome to do so.

But why do we have to yield to grammatical correctness, especially if it creates fuzziness? Personally, I have a hard time grasping the concept of "either" as meaning this side **and** that side. We happen to have a simpler (and in my mind, better) way to express the idea. Just substitute the word "both" for "either," and there's absolutely no ambiguity! "On **both** sides of the ocean" is perfectly clear to everyone, I trust.

So either use "either" to mean "one or the other," or phrase things another way. But try not to use "either" to mean "both this and that." Either you will agree to this, or you won't!

P.S. British/English dictionaries list the pronunciation "eye-ther" first, then "ee-ther." American dictionaries list "ee-ther" first, meaning it is preferred over "eye-ther" on the west side of the Atlantic. Which side of this ocean are you on, if you're on **either** one? (You can't be on both sides at once, can you?)

22

Emphasizing Prepositions

I have a feeling that this "error," if it is one, is pretty well confined to announcers in the media and other public speakers. So persons who don't ordinarily function in such a capacity may move on if they care to. But since public speakers and broadcasters are very much in need of the points explored in this book, we include the caution brought out on this page.

By their very nature, prepositions are not usually the most important words in a sentence. They show connections and relationships among other, more critical words; and most of them are fairly short.

But how frequently we hear announcers land hard on the generally insignificant prepositions "to" and "for"! "We will bring it TO you" is decidedly inferior to "We will **bring** it to you" or "We will bring it to **you**." (Of course, it may be appropriate to say something like "I'm taking this **from** you." There are always exceptions to any generalization. But it's best to place emphasis most of the time on the primary words that convey meaning. This practice also sounds more natural.)

Am I allowed a pet peeve? I get really exasperated when I hear a radio or TV broadcaster come out with "This IS (name of station or channel)." "Is" is a verb, not a preposition, but it also violates our senses and sensibilities when stressed out of all proportion. I don't care to hear what the station or channel was, is, or will be. I'm waiting to hear what its **name** is or what the **call letters** are!

This **is** my best advice **to** you out there **in** the media world. I'll be listening to find out whether it's acted upon!

Errors in Sports

In the summer of 2010, a baseball umpire blew the call on a play that would have been the final out in a perfect game. The umpire later apologized to the pitcher, and the error was forgiven. Errors do happen, also in judgment calls. They are so common because everyone is human and therefore susceptible to mistakes. But thankfully, errors can also be forgiven, and life can go on!

In this book of linguistic errors, I hope it isn't out of place to devote a page to errors in sports. The aim isn't to criticize such errors (they are not a character flaw in the players!) but to highlight the fact that errors are part of life. We needn't be upset by them; rather, we can train ourselves to overcome errors and keep them to a minimum.

One way to go about this sidetrack is merely to call attention to various ways that errors show up in various sports. Space doesn't permit including all of them (who even knows all of them?), so we'll mention only some of the prominent ones:

Basketball – traveling; fouling; double-dribbling; lane violations; goaltending. **Football** – going offside; personal foul; holding; fumbling; interfering with passes; unnecessary roughness. **Baseball** – errors (of course); balks; passed balls; wild pitches; passing another runner; fighting. (But **stealing** is okay, even encouraged!)

Hockey – roughing; slashing; high-sticking; spearing; going offside. **Soccer** – going offside; using hands (except for goalkeeper); illegal tackling; head-butting. **Golf** – slicing; hooking; duffing; going out-of-bounds or into traps and hazards; missing short putts! **Tennis** – hitting the net; hitting out-of-bounds; forced errors; **un**forced errors; double-faulting; missing the ball completely.

I suppose the world itself could not contain all the possible errors. But be cheerful; we can overcome the world if we concentrate on improving!

Feel Bad/Feel Badly

"Badly" is a perfectly **good** adverb. It has its place. "Things are going badly today," we may say. (Sometimes it's "things are going from bad to worse," as in an economic downturn!)

But when "badly" follows the verb "feel," we enter a danger zone. To feel **badly** means to have a poor sense of touch. If your fingers brush up against a hot stove and you're burned before you know it, you're feeling **very** badly. You may have to get some finger therapy so you won't feel so badly in the future.

The **verbal**-zone danger crops up when people complain, as they often do, "I feel badly today." Come again? That's a dead giveaway (or at least an **ill**-chosen giveaway!) that such complainers are unfamiliar with language structure. In this example, "feel" is a linking verb that requires a predicate **adjective** to describe the **person** (a noun) who isn't feeling well. The adverb "badly" is out of place here, because it isn't the **act of feeling** that's being described. So the proper expression is "I feel **bad** today." Sorry about that—doubly so.

Have you ever heard someone say, "I feel **goodly**"? I'm sure I haven't, although it's possible that you may have. Why, we'd think such a statement outlandish! Why, then, do some ill persons unhesitatingly blurt out, "I feel **badly**"? It makes no sense, to me at least.

Speaking of "badly," I recall the cute story about a young girl who decided to call her teddy bear, which was cross-eyed, "**Gladly**." "What a strange name!" remarked the girl's father. "Why did you pick **that** name?"

"It's simple," she replied. "My favorite hymn is 'Gladly the Cross I'd Bear' "!

Feeling Different(ly)

Suppose someone told you, "Tomorrow you'll feel differently." How would you **feel** about that prediction—differently, or different? You'd have to undergo a lot of changes in 24 hours if you were to feel different**ly**! Your hands would need to be smoother or rougher or some other "-er." "Differently" is an adverb and applies to the texture of one's touch or the **means** by which one feels, usually with one's hands.

"Different" is an adjective that describes the mental or emotional state of the **person** doing the feeling. In the sentence at the start of this page, "feel" is a **linking** verb and needs to be followed by an adjective that tells something about "**you**." So if you think **you** will be in a different mood tomorrow, use the adjective "different." But if you think your hands will undergo changes by tomorrow in the way they work (a very remote possibility), use the adverb "differently." **See the difference**?

A test: How would you react to these exact quotes? From a national TV show: "Do you feel differently about living here?" From a national magazine: "By the time of the book's publication, many people may feel differently." For extra credit, rate this sentence: "The doctor told me to think differently about my illness."

Fillet/Filet

Which is correct—one "l" (filet) or two "l's" (fillet)? It all depends! If you go to a supermarket, you're likely to find "fillet of sole" and "fillet mignon" side by side. The perpetrators of these signs don't realize that **filet** (one "l") **mignon** is a French term (literally, "dainty fillet") and thus should be spelled with a **single** "l." Even if you suggest that the managers correct the misspelling, they usually ignore you. They just don't get it!

But no matter how you **slice** them, or fillet them, fillets of fish and filets mignons are both indescribably delicious. I guess people will still buy and eat them, no matter how they're spelled.

Founder/Flounder

Here's a "whopper" that takes the cake, to mix a metaphor! "The nation's economy will continue to **founder**," predicted an expert economist. Now, if the economy has already foundered (that is, failed utterly), how can it **continue** to founder? **Real**ly, are we not getting into the **real**m of the un**real** or the sur**real**?

Perhaps that expert was **floundering** in search of the right verb, which appropriately would have been "**flounder**." There can be a long way to go from floundering (or thrashing about in confusion, a usually temporary activity) to an actual foundering, which is a total and permanent collapse. If we can't trust economists to describe the state of our economy, whom can we trust? Moreover, if our nation's economy **founders**, we may as well "hang it up."

Flounder that **swim**, of course, often flounder in the water before they founder on an angler's rod and reel. But that's the kind of foundering we go for, because then we don't need to **continue floundering** in search of our next meal!

Further/Farther & Fewer/Less

Sometimes there's a very fine distinction between two words that mean essentially the same thing. The **further** along you go in life, the **farther** you may have to go to reach your destination. Assuming that "destination" in that sentence is a physical location, we've just illustrated how "further" and "farther" differ.

"Further" means "to a greater **extent** or degree." "Farther" means "to a more distant **place** or point"—in other words, farther than **far**! So when space scientists brag that "telescopes are now probing **further** into space," we may wonder whether the technology has outstripped the terminology. Likewise, when a chemical company concludes that "the **further north** you go, the less of a problem our chemical has been," we may suspect that they haven't done their linguistic homework. To my knowledge, at least no one has corrupted "furthermore" into "**farther**more"!

Now we come to a pair of vocables known as "fewer" and "less." It's more of a **stretch** than you may imagine to **catch** how much "fewer" is less than "**less**." In fact, I don't really know how few are the minor disparities between "fewer" and "less." Neverthe**less**, it's my best **guess** that it's a **mess** to **stress** the distinctions.

To cut a long soliloquy short, suffice it to say that "fewer" refers to a smaller **number**, and "less" refers to a smaller **amount** or extent (as in "less of a problem," above). To put it another way, "a lot **fewer** people" makes more sense than "a lot **less** people." Or, if you're doing math, 8 is **fewer** than 10, but 10 **less** 8 is 2!

Gel/Gelatin/Jell/Jelly

I'm jealous. Of what? I'm **jeal**ous of people who can spell "gel," "jell," "gelatin," "jellied," "gelatinous," and "jellify," and keep their pronunciations straight. I usually get these similar terms all mixed up, so that causes "autobiographical errors." In fact, when I need to use one of these words, I nearly turn into jelly!

I'm told that gel is a jellylike (!) substance used in styling hair and preparing drugs. It's hard to **swallow** something that you use on your hair!

But I guess that gel**atins** are good to eat. (They have to **jell** first, though.) However, gelatinous proteins obtained from the skin and bones of animals (such as horses) are used in making **glue**. Who wants to taste **that**?

The dictionary reveals that "to jell" is "to cause to become gelatinous." Why couldn't that last word be spelled "jellatinous"? Jelly jells, but gels don't "gell." Things just don't jell for me when the "g's" and "j's" are always dancing jigs (or should that be "gigues"?).

Jellybeans and jellyrolls are good to eat, but I'd stay away from jelly**fish**. Jelly is another popular item, made by boiling sugar with fruit juice and letting the mixture con**geal**. Jolly good! **Petroleum** jelly is another story; you wouldn't want **that** on your plate.

When all is said and done, it's hard to err when we're dealing with gels and jellies. Just remember to keep the "gels" and "jells" apart in your head. I won't be jealous of you if you can do **that** much!

Go Cubs/Go, Cubs
(To Comma or Not to Comma?)

When we talk to someone or address someone in writing, we're using what is called "direct address." In speech, of course, we don't employ punctuation or see it. But in writing we need to observe basic rules of punctuation that contribute to understanding.

For instance, a phrase such as "Go Cubs" **could** mean that the Cubs are a "go-go" team—similar to go-go dancers or even go-carts. They're a team "on the go" (sometimes). But what the fans are really doing is imploring the Cubs **to go**! Therefore, a comma is needed before the persons addressed: "**Go, Cubs**." Then there's no misunderstanding.

The same principle applies in letter writing or other forms of written address. "Hi Mom" just doesn't cut it. Is she on a high? Is she a tall mom? The basic rule we (should have) learned in elementary school applies: Use a comma before addressing someone—thus: "**Hi, Mom**." Also, a comma is in order between such words as "attention" and the addressee(s). This is often overlooked. Furthermore, we place a comma **after** the person(s) addressed when they come first. A sample prayer should begin: "Lord, remember me," not "Lord remember me."

These are fine points, but can they be that hard to recall? Or do we just give in to laziness and ignore the rules, thus watering down our language even more? Hello, everybody! Attention, all aspiring writers! Go, language lovers—and Cubs!

Good/Well

It's all good and well that we have the two words "good" and "well." We need them both, but we would do **well** to know the difference between them. "Good" is usually an adjective that describes a person, place, or thing. "Well" is usually an adverb that tells how something is done. Of course, a good person can also be a **well** person, when "well" means "healthy." But a well person isn't necessarily a **good** person! (Want me to say that again?)

You may have heard a friend moan, "I can't sing very good." Well, that could very well be true, but the sentence isn't good English. Because a verb ("sing") is being modified, it likes to be followed by an **ad**verb. So "well" is the right choice to tell **how** one sings.

Sports announcers sometimes come up with "doozies" such as "He played **real good**." Well? It's the same error as the previous one. But if an announcer were to say, "He played a real good **game**," that would be right-on. The adjective "good" describes the noun "game."

So what's the difference between "well" and "good"? Well, after you've read this far, you should realize that "good" and "well" are **cousins** but not identical **twins**. Good! Let's leave well enough alone!

Harking Back/Hearkening Back

The headline of an editorial column in a big-city newspaper blared: "Harkening to Jim Crow Era." Aside from the fact that the first word of the headline is a variant of the more-common "hearkening," what exactly did the headline mean? **Listening to** a bygone era? Hardly. **Giving heed to** a shameful period in American history? Quite improbable, to judge from the article. The editor at the other end of the call-in line paid no attention to several inquiries. Perhaps he was embarrassed by the apparent goof!

A prominent book publisher also failed to respond to a letter about a still-more-prominent journalist's use of the phrase "hearkening **back**." What's going on here? People are misusing words undoubtedly because they've seen or heard **other** people misusing them. That's how errors get woven into the warp and woof of "wisdom" that is wanting.

The key to this particular riddle is simply that an idiom is in play. The two-word verb "**harking back**" has the specific meaning of "returning to a previous point or time." Evidently, even some well-known authors in the know don't know this. Perhaps they will come across this book. Then maybe the word will spread that "harking back" is correct and "hearkening back" is a faux pas. Hark-hark! What a lark!

"OW! MY HARKING BACK !"

P.S. We can now ascertain that the writer of the aforementioned editorial meant to decry or forestall a possible **return to** a bygone era, though the headline didn't use the right term.

Has Been/Have Been

What do you think? Should the film critic have written: "There **has been** only a handful of hits in the last few years" or "There **have been** only a handful of hits"? One could argue that "handful" is a singular noun and therefore requires a singular verb. But what follows "handful" is **plural**—"of hits"! So shouldn't "have been" have been the right choice?

Would you be caught dead saying, "There **has been** a lot of home runs 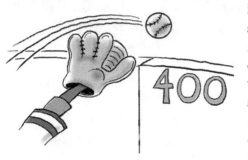 in this game"? I doubt it. So it seems that what **follows** the first noun ("handful"; "lot") determines the number of the verb. In these examples the **second** nouns, "hits" and "home runs" (whoops—is that a coincidence?), are plural; therefore, we **score** with the plural verb in both cases: "have been." There, I guess we hit that one out of the park!

P.S. The film critic used "has been." (Thanks, critic, for supplying fodder for this book.)

Having Said That/That Being Said

To participle or not to participle—that is the question. It makes a large difference whether you begin a sentence with "having said that" or "that being said." What's the difference? Read on!

"Having" is one of those pesky little participles that haunt us. An opening participle has to be linked, joined, or attached to a noun or pronoun that follows it—not just **any** noun or pronoun, but the **right** one. So if you hear something like "Having said that, the meeting is now over," you know something's amiss. "Having" is attached to a noun, "meeting." But did the **meeting** do the "having said"? Obviously not.

"Having said that" must be followed by a pronoun that identifies **who did the saying**—namely, "I," "we," or "she," etc. The sentence is nonsensical—often hilarious, even—if this rule isn't followed (e.g., "Having finished the lecture, the audience left").

On the other hand, "that being said" (or just "that said") can stand alone, without a link to the speaker(s). Why so? Simply because the participle "being" is **already attached** to a pronoun: "that." So if you have to choose between using "having said that" and using "that being said," it's safer to go with the **latter**. Then you won't need to worry about how the sentence should continue.

Having said all that (in writing), **I** now declare the session over!

Help To . . .

Help me! Help me! I don't know how to stop people from wasting a "to." "Help me **to** . . . ; help me **to** . . ." is all I hear and see. Why "to," for Pete's sake (whoever Pete is)? It's way toooo much!

For instance, a prestigious magazine reported: "Innovations have **helped** manufacturers **to** produce and ship goods more efficiently." Now, let's remove that "to" and check the result. The resulting outcome is that innovations have helped manufacturers produce and ship stuff in better ways. Do you see any difference in meaning? I don't. So **help** me.

The truth is, "help" is already enough help by itself. It doesn't need **another** helper, which is what "to" would be if it were needed, which it isn't. (There's probably a better way to put that, if anyone **does** want to help me!)

So please help me out of the pickle I'm in. I'm **too** tired of seeing **two** words used when one is enough without the superfluous "**to**." It's too bad this happens. Enough already!

Highest of Any/Highest of All

Please help with making sense of such expressions as "highest of **any**." Practically everyone uses them without giving them a second thought. But if you **do** give them a second thought, you may have second thoughts about using them!

The problem is this: "Highest" is an indication of ascending degree. It's called a **superlative** because it exceeds all other things it's compared with. So it presupposes a plural number of essences (at least three), of which it is the greatest. However, "**any**" is **singular**. So how can a plural be compared with a singular? That is the dilemma.

An excellent solution is to change "any" to "all" so that plural goes with plural. Thus the sentence "The U.S. once had the highest graduation rate of **any** nation" would instead conclude with "of **all** nations." Another possibility is to convert the superlative degree to a comparative degree: "The U.S. once had a high**er** graduation rate than any **other** nation." (Note the necessary addition of "other.")

This may seem like nitpicking, but it's actually an appeal to reason and logic. The more precise we can be, the more clearly we will be understood. For instance, isn't it more logical to state that love is "the highest of all virtues" rather than "the highest of any virtue"? If the order of words were flipped, how awkward it would sound to hear: "Of **any virtue**, love is the highest"! End of dilemma.

Historic/Historical

Here's an interesting paradox to consider: Every historic event is **historical**, but not every historical event is **historic**. Some commentators confuse the two terms—they may refer to an earthshaking occurrence as a historical (pray, not "**an** historical") happening. But that is also true of all **other** events that take place in the world.

So to designate a particular occasion or happening as especially significant, we employ the more explicit term **historic**. Something stands out in history above other, more mundane affairs. This is history with an "IC" to it—the "HIC effect." The writing and signing of the U.S. Declaration of Independence wasn't merely a historical occurrence, though it indeed happened in history. But beyond that, it was truly **historic**, for reasons most of us are aware of.

P.S. Please **be**ware of using "an" before "historic" or "historical." Consonant sounds at the beginning of a word are to be preceded by the indefinite article "a," not "an," unless you happen to make an exception, as the British do in this case. Surely no one would say, for instance, "**An** history of America"!

Homing in/Honing In

I hope you're feeling **sharp** (not "sharply") today. We're going to discuss the difference between "homing in" and "honing in." There seems to be a bit of confusion regarding these very similar expressions.

No doubt you know what **homing pigeons** do. Whether carrying messages or not, they go for **home**. After roaming far and wide, they "home in" on their place of origin. Have you ever heard of a "**honing** pigeon"? Neither have I. So why do some folks slip into the error of saying or writing "**honing** in"?

As a substitute for "homing in," "honing in" belongs in **Dulls**ville! To "hone" means to **sharpen**, so how do you "sharpen **in**" on something? Yet this screwy phrase still appears in prominent places.

Consider this malapropism gleaned from a highly respected magazine: "While other authors have treated this subject in various ways, (name) **hones in** on another thread." (I assume the author meant "**zeroes** in.") In the very same issue, "homes in" occurred correctly. What's going on? Editors, make up your mind! Do you need to **sharpen** your vision so that you "hone in" on the right spelling?

I think I'll stick to homing in on my own home. That way I won't have to worry about honing my wits concerning the correctness of "homing in" or "honing in." And I'll shave with the sharpest edges ever homed—whoa; make that **honed**, honey!

However

It seems that the prevailing practice concerning the use of "however" is to place it in the middle (not "midst") of a sentence. Some authorities even claim that "however" **must** go there rather than at the sentence beginning.

However, several factors suggest that the start of a sentence is the **optimal** location for "however":

1. This position avoids an awkward interruption in the body of a sentence. Read aloud: "It must, however, be pointed out," and see how disjointed the words sound. "However, it must be pointed out" comes out much smoother.
2. A "however" at the start **alerts** the reader or listener to the **type of sentence** that's coming, just as words like "although" and "nevertheless" do. Otherwise, the reader/listener is in the dark until reaching the point where "however" occurs.
3. Last but not least, only one comma is required, not two. Thus a space is saved, as well as a small amount of energy, paper, etc. Isn't conservation the "in thing" now?

Can "**however**" ever be first? And how!

P.S. This same reasoning could apply to the desirability of placing "for example" and "for instance" in the opening position. However, variation in word order is also desirable.

I Would Like to/I Want To

One of the most useful tools in an editor's toolbox is called "tightening." This refers to removing unnecessary or extraneous words from an author's manuscript. In an age when time and resources are increasingly at a premium, it's disturbing to waste paper, printer's ink or computer wear-and-tear, and brain/hand/voice energy (let alone time) on excess verbiage.

Consider the following, a typical example that occurs frequently: "I would like to take this opportunity to express my sincere appreciation for . . . " (whatever the favor has been). Though we can't point to a specific grammatical error here, the mind of the recipient staggers to take in such a grandiose pronouncement: 12 words when only one would suffice—"Thanks"!

Why tell someone what you'd **like** to do or **want** to do? Just do it! Isn't **every** moment or space an opportunity? Delete "take this opportunity"! Get right **to the point** without riffing about "expressing sincere appreciation"! In other words, TIGHTEN. Other people will be glad you did. And you will have conserved valuable resources to boot.

P.S. Maybe you can practice tightening this rather lengthy put-down.

If I Was/If I Were

Undoubtedly you have heard or sung the song, a children's favorite, "If I Were a Butterfly." Why do we sing "If I were" rather than "If I was"? That's because children (as well as grownups) are **not** butterflies. So we move from the indicative mood (the way things are) to the **subjunctive** mood (the way things **could** be or the way we'd **like** them to be). Thus the switch from "was" to "were."

A lot of "if clauses" are followed by the verb "were," but only if the "ifs" are untrue or hypothetical. If the "if clause" is true (factual), then "was" is the right verb—for example, "If I was with you yesterday (as I'm sure I was), then I wasn't alone." But the common saying **"If I was you"** is always wrong! (I **can't** be you.)

A famous TV interviewer recently came out with this boo-boo: "If this bill was in effect in 1995, things would be better today." But the bill was **not** in effect in 1995, so the interviewer should have said, "If this bill **had been** in effect in 1995 . . . ." ("Had been" corresponds to the subjunctive form "were," but in the past tense.)

P.S. **If I were** you (but I'm not), I wouldn't be so "iffy" about being a butterfly. I'd get up and **fly**, like a sweet little **butter**cup!

42

Insure/Ensure

Are you sure you know the difference between "insure" and "ensure"? I can assure you that many persons don't appear to have a clue. It's quite common to see or hear appeals such as "We can **insure** that you'll be safe if you use our product."

Does such a claim mean that the advertisers are offering an **insurance** policy to go along with their product? That isn't a **sure bet**! Little do they realize that customers would be surer to buy the item if they could trust the ad-makers to spell and use words correctly. (An aside: Studying and absorbing the material in this book can help you become a more discerning shopper!)

"**In**sure" means to guarantee that a sum of money will be paid or a product will be replaced if it turns out faulty. "**En**sure" means to guarantee that a company stands behind its promises and will surely honor all terms and conditions of a sale.

So the best way to **ensure** that customers will be happy is to **insure** products against defects or loss—that is, to provide an insurance policy that will pay off if something bad or unforeseen happens. And if you are the buyer, assuredly the best policy is to be sure you are getting adequate "**en**surance" to go along with sufficient **in**surance coverage!

Inter/Intern

Would you rather be inter**r**ed or inter**n**ed? There is a difference—a **huge** difference. That little "n" instead of an "r" is the difference between life and death. Recall some words of Shakespeare: "The good is oft interred with their bones." "In**terred**" means to be confined in the ground: buried. "In**terned**" means to be confined in a secure place, as in a jail. (Remember this the next time you read that a deceased person is going to be "interned.")

Neither prospect, interment or internment, is especially desirable. But at least an interned person has some hope of escaping quick interment. However, I once knew an intern (different meaning: a person in training) who was first interned, and then, in turn, interred. There was no more escape or hope for him!

P.S. One way to distinguish these two words is to be aware that the Latin word *terra* (as in "terra firma") means earth or ground. Thus, "in terra" equals "in the ground."

Iterate/Reiterate

Do you know the meaning of the word "iterate"? I will repeat that: Do you know what "iterate" means? Maybe I should **re**iterate that. Whoa—let's go back and redo all this!

If you look up "iterate," you'll find that it means "to say again; repeat." If you look up "**re**iterate," you'll find that it means "to say again; repeat." (Avoid "repeat again," which would be redundant.) Do I need to repeat this, or do you get the gist?

I **don't** get it. Why do we **need** both these words? Aren't they also a redundancy, a duplication? It's like the old joke about two guys named Pete and Repeat, who were sitting on a fence. So I'll make up a similar one that repeats the punch line. "Iterate and Reiterate were sitting on a fence. Iterate fell off. Who was left?" Answer: "Reiterate." Continue: "Iterate and Reiterate were sitting on a fence . . . ."

Oh, well, I'm sure you get the gist by **now**. That's just the gist of this whole put-on—or should I call it a "knock**off** "? Okay, okay; I'll knock if off now!

It's Me/It's I

A star baseball player once said, "I had a warm feeling, but it wouldn't have been **me**." He was referring to the fact that he didn't care to acknowledge the crowd's loud cheering after they had witnessed one of his towering home runs.

We're getting into a gray area here. Technically, "it" followed by "me" after a verb such as "is" or "would have been" is incorrect. A pronoun used in the subjective position likes to be linked with **another** subjective-case pronoun. In other words, the correct wording would be "It is **I**" or "It would have been **I**."

Think of the biblical story of Jesus' walking on water. Did he tell the fearful fishermen, who thought they were seeing a ghost, "It is me"? No, Jesus knew correct grammar! His calming assurance was "It is **I**."

However, in informal speech and writing, people commonly resort to "It's me." This expression is easier to spout, and it may sound more natural. But if you were writing a novel or a short story, you surely wouldn't come out with "You're a better person than **me am**, Gunga Din." You would use the grammatically correct and better-sounding "You're a better person than **I am**."

So if I were training students to write well, or speakers to speak well, I would recommend striving to be right **all the time**. It isn't "me" who's advising this advice; it's **I**!

Just Deserts/Just Desserts

If you happen to dislike desserts (of whatever kind), you will tend to desert them. Then you will be getting your "**just deserts**." But if you were deserted in a **desert**, you would possibly think you **deserved** some desserts. In that case, you could be served your "**just desserts**." Get it? I hope so; otherwise, you could starve.

Most of the time the appropriate phrase is "just deserts" (one "s" in the middle), since very few of us spend time in deserts, where desserts would be especially welcome. So if someone tells you in writing that you are getting your "just desserts," just (there's that word again) remind them that you really want what you **deserve** (the base word for "deserts," with only one "s" in the center).

Of course, if you actually deserved to be deserted in a desert, you would indeed be happy just to receive your just desserts!

Kind/Kinds & Type/Types

We'll try to be kind to people who become a bit confused when they want to use the word "kind." An anonymous quotation in my file goes like this: "It's going to take more exertion to win the **kind of victories** we want to win."

What's wrong with that assertion? The boldface words are a clue. The **singular** noun "kind" is joined with the **plural** noun "victories." That's only a slight mistake, but a mistake nonetheless. We combine apples with apples, so we should also combine singulars with singulars, and plurals with plurals. The edited phrase would be either "kind of victory" or "kinds of victories." I hope that's kind enough to the originator of the quote.

Something like this happens when a demonstrative adjective **precedes** "kind" or "type." Often we hear or see such expressions as "those kind of stories" and "these type of laws." The same principle applies: Join singulars together and plurals together. So we end up with "these **types** of laws" and "**that** kind of **story**."

It's all about logic. Logical thinking helps us steer clear of illogical terms and expressions. I kind of like the kinds of improvements we make when we use our minds in kindly ways, like keeping "kind" and "kinds" in kinder constraints!

Kind of a/A Half of a

Sometimes a goose may get too loose with its honking. Similarly, writers and speakers may get too loose with extra "a's," honking them out in a steady stream and leading **other** writers and speakers to follow them.

What is an extra "a"? It's an unnecessary word inserted after phrases like "sort of," "kind of," and "half of." Exhibit A: "What **kind of a** world does China hope to shape?" wrote a prominent journalist. That's a little "loosey-goosey," in my opinion. Take **out** the extra "a," and we have "What **kind of** world?" Ah, that's better—and we've "saved" another **letter**!

Exhibit B: "The plumber detected some **sort of a** leak in the pipes." It's a pipe dream to think you need an extra "a" after "some sort of." We can plug that leak by **un**plugging the word "a," which leaves us with "some sort of leak." (Maybe our "plugging" also avoids an expensive repair bill!)

Exhibit C: "Retail sales declined by **a half of a** percent." Wow! Here we have **two** "a's." Can we delete one of them? Why, certainly (not "absolutely"). We could go with either "half a percent" or "a half percent." Please note that we **also** dropped an extra "of." We're getting more economical all the time!

If a goose can get by with a little less honking, we can surely do with fewer "a's" and "of's"—**can't** we? (Notice how "less" and "fewer" played out there—see page 29.)

Lead/Led

Most people are aware that lead (pronounced "**led**") is a metal used in many products. Thus, this "lead" is a noun. But there's also a verb spelled the same way, though pronounced "**leed**." This "lead" means "to guide." To complicate matters, the past tense of the verb "lead" is spelled and pronounced "**led**." So, do two "leads" make a "led," or do two "leds" make a "lead"? That's certainly a **leading** question!

Why is it that so often we see the past tense of the verb "lead" spelled LEAD instead of LED, as in the sentence "The group **lead** the audience in singing"? Maybe it's because we have learned to spell the **noun** as L-E-A-D, so when we need to use the **verb** "led," we spell it as we would the noun "lead."

But we have to get the lead **out** when we want to write "led." Otherwise, we'll be leading further astray those folks who are led to write "**lead**" for "led"!

Does this lead you in the right direction?

Lie/Lay

"Why don't you go and lay down?" she asked. Lay **what** down? My head? My lei? Such a question is ambiguous, to say the least. If an object of "lay" is intended, the object needs to be supplied and the verb form may stand. But if no object is intended, the verb form is incorrect. The questioner should have used the **intransitive** (without an object) verb "lie": "Why don't you go and **lie** down?"

I'm not lying when I say that "lie" and "lay" are probably the most misused or misunderstood verbs in English. Seriously, I've seen serious books that get them confused all the way through! One reason could be that "lay" is the **past** tense of "lie" as well as the **present** tense of "lay." So the sequence of tenses goes: "lie–lay–have lain" and "lay–laid–have laid."

To say something like "I laid down" is to lay an egg. But I will lay you odds that laying down the law about using "lie" and "lay" correctly may get you laid into by laypersons who lie in wait in the secret lairs of their self-imposed layers of defense mechanisms. (Just kidding!)

Like/As

Is "like" a conjunction? Not ordinarily, like it or not. It's usually a preposition or a verb or an adjective—or sometimes even a noun. So when we start using "like" like a conjunction, we may get into trouble.

How often haven't you heard or said, "Like I said"? That comes across as somewhat jarring to the trained ear. In fact, one dictionary cautions that using "like" in such a way borders on illiteracy! (Disclaimer: In rapid conversation, things like "like I said" may slip out unintentionally or out of habit from hearing **others** use the phrase habitually. But that doesn't make the usage correct.)

Can we, like (sorry about that!), train ourselves to substitute the proper conjunctions "as" or "as if" when "like" is inappropriate? How much more pleasing it would be to others if we said or wrote or entered "**as** I said" and "I felt **as if** I were being lied to"! Try it—you'll **like** it! (And so will the "others.")

P.S. To impress the distinction between "like" and "as" upon your mind all the more, imagine how odd it would sound to hear a church choir sing: "Just **like** I am, without one plea"!

Long "a"/Short "a"

I think I've heard all the long "a's" I ever want to hear. How many speakers and announcers, when they meet that trivial little vowel, consistently and stubbornly come out with "Ayyyyy"! And they will probably do it for **aye**. It's "ayyy" board, "ayyy" job, "ayyy" credit card, *ad infinitum* (Latin for "into infinity"). Don't they realize that this offensive habit offends hearers who know better, and really hangs out?

All they have to do is look in the dictionary just once. They will discover that the correct pronunciation is the **short "a"**—"uh, uh, uh"! Say it till you're blue in the face: "uh, uh, uh." Why put such strong emphasis on the shortest and most insignificant word in our language? It's just plain silly to use the long "a"—unless, of course, you're saying your A-B-C's or want to add stress to this vowel. Then the long option is admissible—for instance: "I said it was '**ayyy**' year, not **many** years."

A final reminder: The **overuse** of stress (as in the habitual, never-varying use of long "a's") results in **nothing** being stressed or the inability to employ stress when really needed. And isn't "uh man" a bit easier to say, and a bit easier on the listener's ear, then the sharp crack of "ayyy man"? Try switching to the short "a"; you may like it, **eh**?

Mantle/Mantel

A sales clerk in a furniture store was demonstrating various ways to decorate a living room. When she came to the fireplace, she showed photos of different arrangements for the mantel. But the captions on the photos referred to the shelf of the fireplace as the "**mantle**."

Perhaps no one other than the late Mickey Mantle, of New York Yankee fame, would have been offended at such a slip-up. But still, there were a few muffled chuckles as the photos made the rounds of the spectators. It isn't a major blunder to confuse a **mantel** with a **mantle** (a cloak). But it could lead some of a store's prospective customers to question the trustworthiness of the personnel.

According to the sales clerk, **candles** on mantels are great handles for decorating fireplaces. But suppose that someone, for some reason, spread a concealing **mantle** over a mantel. If so, could a **man tell** it was a mantel? Great question, huh?

Of course, to **dis**mantle a mantel of its "mantle" of popularity would be ill-advised. So be careful about "cloaking" your love of fancy mantels with a dismantling display of distasteful doodads!

P.S. True story: Once an artist was hired to draw the prophet Elisha carrying the trusty mantle of his teacher, Elijah, who had gone to heaven. Not being well acquainted with the Bible, the artist submitted a sketch of Elisha lugging a huge **mantel** on his back!

Many, Many & Very, Very

It's **very** difficult to know how **many** times the combinations "many, many" and "very, very" appear. It would take a wordsmith working "many, many" years to document the frequency of such occasions. The task would very likely never get finished unless "very, very" many estimates and projections were made.

The reason is simple: These repetitive (and therefore **redundant**) combinations **flow forth** in seemingly endless **streams**, presumably also when "streaming" is happening (isn't that nearly all the time?). What do speakers and writers and texters think they're accomplishing when they tack "many" onto "many," and "very" onto "very"? Evidently, they're trying to add (or multiply?) emphasis by doubling the words. But is that really necessary? Do two or three, or even **four**, "manys" increase the number of the many things being counted? Do very many "verys" make a thing more "**varied**" (excuse the flimsy pun)?

What's **really** happening is that people are falling back onto clichés! They get into the thoughtless practice of repeating phrases they've **very** likely heard **many** times before. So buck the trend and find **vari**ous other ways to add (or multiply) emphasis. You'll be very glad you did, many times over (and—I'm sorry—over and over and over again)!

P.S. Many years ago (more than 60) my father humorously imitated speakers who were partial to "very, very" and "many, many." So I felt emboldened by family tradition to point out these excesses here.

May/Might

It's helpful to get something straight right away: "May" and "might" are not two completely separate words that are interchangeable in meaning. Most persons use them that way, blissfully unaware that "might" is (ordinarily, at least) the **past tense** of "may." Surprise! "May" is the preferred word in almost all instances, except when the action or dialogue occurs in the past. That shouldn't be too hard to remember.

I realize that some "purists" insist that "may" gives permission whereas "might" indicates a possibility. "May" does indeed grant permission; but it may **also** signal possibility, may it not? (I just used it twice in that sense.) "You may go there" could have two distinct meanings: "You have permission to go there" or "You possibly will go there." So the purists' argument is beside the point. In this case, "might" doesn't always make **right**.

Once the truth is known about past and present tenses in this context, "might" starts to grate on a person when consistently used in the present tense, as it so often is. Think this way: "I **might** have done that yesterday, but I **may** do it today." However, we won't be so rigid as to nix the familiar rhyme "I wish I may; I wish I might . . . ." After all, poetry is a world unto itself!

Me/My

During a Congressional hearing, an official in the President's cabinet uttered this sentence: "It had nothing to do with me becoming Secretary." What's wrong with that? Nothing, it appears. But wait! Did the speaker really mean "it" (whatever "it" was) had nothing to do with **him personally**? Or was the real point that he had **become Secretary** of some department, and that "it" had nothing to do with **that fact**? Upon closer examination, we find that the latter case was true.

Therefore, the official should have said, "It had nothing to do with **my** becoming Secretary." The **possessive** form of the pronoun was in order, for that would have placed the emphasis where it actually belonged: on the "becoming," not on the "me." This same principle applies in many other instances, so "a word to the wise is sufficient." My, my!

P.S. Could someone please explain why many British persons say "ME mother" instead of "MY mother"? Why is "my" seemingly AWOL or even frowned upon as a possessive pronoun? A prize awaits the best responder!

Mismatches with Antecedents

There's no lack of examples for **this** example of straying off the beaten path. All I have to do is start rattling off some of the most egregious (and often hilarious) quotes I've collected, and you'll catch on quickly.

"When in a state of anxiety, my education doesn't help me." (This says that the **education** is anxious!)

"As a Rewards cardmember, **we** invite you . . . ." ("**We**"—the credit-card company—are the **member**! Illogical? Very.)

"As a leader, your ongoing support allows us to . . . ." (The **support** is the leader! Goodness gracious!)

"As governor, **allow me** to welcome you." ("You," the understood subject of "allow me," are the governor! What an instant promotion!)

You get the picture. Further examples would be superfluous; you yourself can find them all over the place.

What's the solution to all such gibberish? Simply determine whether the main subject agrees with or matches what has gone before it (the **ante**cedent). If there's a mismatch, the sentence has to be restructured. For instance, the governor in example four could have pleaded, "Allow **me as governor** to welcome you." Then there would have been no ambiguity.

Best wishes on matching up with your "auntie-cedents." It's a fascinating game to play—even moreso if you emerge victorious!

P.S. Here's a pop quiz (it's for moms and kids too): How would you respond to this quote from an ad put out by an insurance company: "As parents of young children, life insurance is key"?

My Own Personal . . .

What a divergence was created by the newscaster who intoned, "There's a **divergence** between his **own personal** popularity and his policies"! That's one way to divert listeners: Distract them from one's message by rendering a redundancy.

What's the difference between "own" and "personal"? Very little, if any (besides the spelling and pronunciation). If we **own** up to it, what is our **own** is also our **personal** possession or attribute. So we don't need to use both words; either one is quite enough. They are **not** Siamese twins, if you know what I mean (never one without the other).

If I sell you my own house, it's also my personal dwelling. It belongs to no one else until I convey it to you—**in deed**! My **person** is involved in the transfer. What I owned is now **your** personal possession, so you own it now.

I wish I could be more personal about all this, but it's my own belief (as well as my **personal** belief) that the cliché "my own personal" belongs in the dustbin of our very own language—which is also our personal treasure, not to be diluted by redundancies!

Myself Included/How's Yourself?

It seems as if the whole world (or at least the English-speaking world) thinks it's okay to use the phrases "myself included" or "including myself." People say things like "The whole town is against this policy, **myself included**." Perhaps they suppose that every time they refer to themselves, they need to use the word "myself."

Not so! The simple truth is that "myself" is **not** a stand-alone substitute for the personal pronouns "I" or "me." Words like "myself," "yourself," and "ourselves" are correctly used only in a **reflexive** or **intensive** sense. (Reflexive sense: "I bought this coat **for myself** "; intensive sense: "**I myself** bought this coat.")

Think like this: I, as a person, am not a "myself"; I'm an "I." Would we say, "**Myself** is going to the store"? Of course not. So why do so many persons insist on using "myself included"? The right course is to use the **personal** pronoun, either as subject ("**I** included") or as object ("including **me**"). So "include me out" from saying "myself included"!

Similarly, if someone asks how you are, please try not to reply, "I'm fine—how's **yourself**?" Practice replying, "I'm fine—how are **you**?" But if someone asks **you**, "How's yourself?" you could respond (if you wanted to be impertinent), "My body's fine, but my **self** is terrible!" That may get the point across, but at the risk of risking your friendship. (You could **think** it, though!) "To thine own **self** be true," as you may have read in *Hamlet*.

Nuclear/Nucular & Cavalry/Calvary

"Nuke-You-Lar"

As inconceivable as it may seem, some persons either cannot or will not pronounce "**nuclear**" correctly. They flip the "l" till later in the word and substitute a "u" for the "e," thus blurting out the strange-sounding "**nucular**." You'd think someone would sit down with them and practice saying "nu-cle-ar" accurately so they wouldn't sound pe-cu-li-ar. But perhaps we should just be charitable and consider them a different kind of "-cular": namely, "**avun**cular"!

And what about the radio announcers (and perhaps others) who insist on pronouncing the famous "Light **Cavalry** Overture" as "Light **Calvary** Overture"? (This sometimes happens even after the broadcasters have been advised of their error.) Wow! It's quite a **gallop** from a group of horse riders to the **mount** on which Jesus was put to death. Would these same speakers also say "**Cagalry**" instead of "**Calgary**" (in Canada)? If so, they would have a hard time qualifying for a job with the Royal Canadian Mounted Police!

Older Than Her/Older Than She

(This item is similar to the "It's Me/It's I" conundrum examined earlier in this book.)

It's very common to hear or see others make comparisons like "He's **older than her**." People are "doin' what comes natcherly," I suppose. "Older than her" may look right. It may sound right. It may **feel** right. But it's regarded by most linguists as **wrong**.

Why, oh, why? Because "he" is being compared with (not "compared **to**") someone else, that someone must be in the **same case** (subjective). "Than" in **this** case isn't a preposition that would require its object to be in the objective case (as "her" would be). Here, "than" is actually a **conjunction** that introduces an **entire clause**, but one that's cut short or abbreviated. What's **understood** after "He's older than" is "**she is old**"—whether she's old or not old! (She could be only one year old and still fit into the comparison, right? "He" could be **two** years old.)

So if you're a boy or a man and your age is being estimated in relation to a younger girl or woman, hope and pray that the estimator will correctly announce, "**He's** older than **she**." Now we're talking real English!

P.S. Please also avoid **starting** a sentence with a wrong "her," as in "Her and Josie are going to the store." That's putting a subject into the **objective** case, which is definitely **objection**able. (Would you say, "Her is going to the store"? Unimaginable. So why would you switch to "her and Josie"? Stick with "**She** and Josie"!)

On a _____ Basis

Now for the granddaddy (four "d's") of all useless phrases: "On a (blah-blah) basis." Why do we so often (or "on a regular basis"!) substitute **four** words for **one** perfectly adequate term? Nothing's gained by that, and a lot is wasted.

I, for one, can't fathom how "on a daily basis" differs from or extends the idea of "daily." Yet I hear this expression on **almost** a daily basis—oops, I mean **daily**. (See how easy it is to slip into annoying habits!) Even "every day" would be preferable to "on a daily basis," don't you think? Similarly, "as a volunteer" would serve us better than "on a volunteer basis."

We also encounter such phrases as "on a monthly basis," "on a yearly basis," and "on a regular basis," ad nauseam. Why can't we be satisfied with "monthly," "yearly," and "regularly"? I file my tax forms **annually**, not **on an annual basis**, because I don't understand what a basis is in this context without a long explanation.

If we're mindlessly going to convert every adverb into a four-word (and, really, **back**ward) prepositional phrase, I suppose "basically" would morph into "on a **basic basis**." Heavens! I propose that we go back to the basics and ban "on a (fill in the blank) basis" to the boondocks. Wouldn't you **basically** agree?

Only/Just

There's a whole family of words that can change the meaning of a sentence by their place or position in the word order. Two of these words are "only" and "just." We'll just tackle "only" first. Or we'll tackle just "only" at first. (I guess you can **only** guess **just** where this is heading!)

Consider this advice given in print by a well-known woman to millions of readers: "Only wear pantyhose when absolutely necessary." Hello? If you saw only (not "only saw") the first three words with a quick glance, you might be shocked all the way to your twinkle-toes. **Only wear pantyhose**, and nothing else? My! What a sight! Now switch "only" to where it should have gone: "Wear pantyhose **only when absolutely necessary**." That's a much more modest suggestion!

A book called *Short Cuts* [*sic*] *to Effective English* posits the position of "only" in seven different places in the sentence "My friend sold his car last week." Try this experiment yourself by inserting "only" in seven different places, and see what the different meanings are. Vive la différence! What a "vas(t) deferens"!

The book goes on to list a number of other words ("troublemakers") that have to be put exactly where they belong to avoid confusion. Among these are "hardly," "almost," "nearly," "alone," and "just." **Just think** of the difference between "I am **just visiting** you today" and "I am visiting you **just today**" (or even "**Just I** am visiting you").

(I alone am only just pulling your leg nearly off!)

Outside of/Off of/Inside Of

"We see ourselves as outside of the mainstream." "The opposing team had eight hits off of our pitcher." "I'll meet you inside of your office." Can you detect the common fault in these three sentences?

The word "**of**" kind **of** sticks out, doesn't it? That's  because it's totally unnecessary. Why put two prepositions together when one will do just fine? "We are **outside** the mainstream." "They had eight hits **off** our pitcher." "I'll join you **inside** your office."

The abbreviated sentences even sound better! Besides, the omission of a superfluous word saves paper and ink (or breath and energy). Keep it simple, to shorten a slogan with four capital letters!

Of course, certain constructions do call for a double preposition. Here's one: "**Outside of** a few insiders, no one knows the secret code." And **you** will be an insider if you know the difference between "outside" and "outside of," and when to use one or the other.

So get **off** your comfy beanbag, and jump **out of** your lethargy. Think **outside** the box, and you will be **outside of** the "hoi polloi" (a Greek expression meaning "the common people").

Over and Over Again/All Over Again

That little word "again" can be quite pesky. Why, oh, why, do we throw it in whenever and wherever it suits us, without giving a thought to its uselessness?

For instance, what's the difference in meaning between the phrases "over and over" and "over and over  again"? None, really, except that adding "again" tends to **double** the effect (whether we **in**tend to or not): First an action takes place over and over; then it happens over and over **some more** ("again")!

Someone has even questioned why the Apostles' Creed of the Christian church states: "He rose **again** from the dead." Did Jesus actually rise from the dead **twice**, as implied by "again"? We'll let the theologians explain that.

Other cases of a similar nature are the phrases "start over **again**" and "all over **again**." One commentator on TV gushed, "We go and do the cycle all over again." Try leaving "all over" out of that sentence, or try omitting "again." Voilà! In both instances the meaning is the same, but we've managed to save space, ink or breath, and time—again!

Part/A Part

Does the word "part" refer to a portion of a thing or to the whole thing? Stupid question, right? So far, so good.

Second question: Does the word "a" refer to a portion of something or to all of it? Hmm. I guess "a book" would refer to a whole book, unless we're talking about a whole **lot** of books. (A **big** lot would hold quite a lot!) Usually we reserve the word THE for the entire sum or essence of what we have in mind. Thus, "**the** book" or "the stack of books" is far more inclusive than "**a** book" or "a stack of books."

So what? Well, let's put "a" and "part" together. That's what we meet most of the time. Examples: "A part of me doesn't like that"; "When a part of the brain dies . . . ." Since "part" is part of a whole, and "a" is usually part of a larger essence, do we really need **both** "a" and "part" together?

I, for one, don't think so. Because "part" **already** refers to part of a whole, "**a part**" is actually redundant! "Part of me" is just as adequate as "a part of me." So why don't we simply drop "a" from "part" and go with the one word "part"? Besides—and this is the key factor—we avoid confusing "a part" and "**apart**"!

There's a big difference between saying, "I want to be apart from the team" and "I want to a part of the team." But if we're talking **fast**, "a part" and "apart" can fly past the listener so rapidly that the terms are hard to **tell** apart.

So why not try separating "a" from "part" to see if your meaning isn't clearer? I'm sure that **part of me** will like it!

P.S. I wouldn't call this a major error, but several minor ones can **make** a major.

Peaked/Peeked/Piqued

I'm piqued (provoked or irritated) that I've lost a newspaper clipping that included the word "peaked" where "peeked" should have gone. But if this error happened once, as it did, it has probably happened more than once. So maybe I (and you too) will come across this mistake again sometime.

If you've ever peeked into a grammar book, you've no doubt come across examples of how words like "peak," "peek," and "pique" get twisted around. It piques (arouses) my curiosity to know how the homonyms "peak" and "peek" got started and why they continue in common parlance. I dare not peek too much; else I'll reach the peak of my frustration and stay piqued for a long time. Hey, even mountains know what it's like to be peaked!

I've just about peaked now in how far I want to go with this piquing (interesting) and piquant (stimulating and exciting) inquiry. So I'll close with a "no-peekin' " observation of how "Pekins" (citizens of **Pekin**, IL) can arrive at the peak of popularity. All they have to do is peek at peaks and never feel **piqued** or look **peak**-ed (sickly).

I myself was born near Pekin, so I classify myself as Pekin**ese**, though I can't speak a word of **Peking**ese, a Chinese dialect! (Pardon me while I pull my tongue out of my cheek. That habit always dogs me.)

Pejorative Use of "Shrink"

This book wouldn't be complete without at least one reference to terms that are intrinsically negative or pejorative. These terms can be classified as "errors" because they are insensitive and are often harmful to the subjects referred to. So the persons **using them** are in serious error.

Here's a quote from someone very much in the public eye: "I'm a politician, **not a shrink**." What was the intent of that disparaging remark? We can't be sure, but a possible effect was to perpetuate a false idea about a class of professional people who provide positive products to promote the personal protection of their patients. For shame, you politician! You succeeded only in tarnishing your own image as a righteous servant of the public.

Such slurs can do damage to a highly reputable group of public servants (in this case, psychiatrists and psychologists). The image formed in people's minds by the term "shrink" is that of doctors who use unscrupulous incantations to manipulate their patients' brains. That in turn may cause very ill persons to avoid treatments that could greatly benefit them. What a **dis**service!

Words do matter. They can have positive or negative effects. We've stopped talking about "ivory-tower professors," haven't we? So why can't we eliminate other tired clichés such as "shrink"? I've seen a national magazine use this term straight-up, without apology. Isn't it about **time** for an apology? Otherwise, the result may be a **shrinking** base of subscribers!

People's/Peoples'

A highly regarded national magazine once referred to "important issues affecting peoples' lives." Do you catch the flaw? The writer was correct in recalling the rule that **plural** possessives are formed by adding an apostrophe after the final "s." But in this case (an exception), "people" is already plural and has no final "s." So the correct spelling for the possessive is "**people's**." Adding "s-apostrophe" after "people" would make the word look unnatural.

However, we can envision an instance when "peoples' " **would** be appropriate. As a synonym for "nations," the word "peoples" would require an apostrophe **after** the "s" to express possession. Here's an example: "The **People's** Republic of China believes in all **peoples'** [that is, nations'] right to govern themselves." (You can debate the truth of that statement.)

So whether you are one of "the people" or whether your country is one of "the peoples" of the world, be careful where you place the apostrophe to indicate possession!

Poem/"Pome"

"How do you like my 'pome'?"

Imagine! Actors on television were reciting poems (two syllables) by Emily Dickinson and calling them "**pomes**" (one syllable). Poor Emily! She would probably have turned over in her grave if she had heard her poems called "pomes."

This error might (past tense of "may") have been excused had it not been for the high pedigree of those who were doing the honors. As it was, they brought **dis**honor on themselves—and embarrassment to many listeners.

Do people actually consult dictionaries (online or off-line) anymore? That's usually the way we determine how words are to be pronounced. I have yet to find a dictionary that shows "poem" as one syllable. (Would "pomes"—if there were such—be written by "**potes**"?)

Students in school, as well as other learners (all of us), would do well to keep a good dictionary within easy reach or to search the Internet regularly (not "on a regular basis," please). That would go a long way toward becoming more familiar with word meanings, spellings, and pronunciations. It would also help us avoid embarrassing slip-ups.

P.S. If you need help getting started, "poem" begins with "p"!

Principal/Principle

A spell-check won't help you in choosing the right word here, if you need to choose one or the other, because "principal" and "principle" are spelled correctly. These are **homonyms**, words that sound alike ("homo") but have different meanings.

Suppose you received a letter from a **high**-ranking institution of **high**er learning, a letter that referred to a visiting professor as "our principle presenter." (I have such a letter in my files.) What would you have thought? The professor might have been a presenter of **principles** (rules or standards); in that case the key word would have been right. But no, the guest speaker was actually the **main** presenter—that is, the **principal** presenter! He might even have been a **school** principal at one time: the **chief** official.

(An aside: Let's be kind and assume that the assistant who prepared that letter did use a spell-check and thought "principle" looked right. But a higher-up of the highly rated institution should have **checked** the letter before it was sent out.)

The principal pitfall of principles is that they're often hard to live up to. Even **princes** don't always follow their principles! Principally, that's because princes, and principals as well, have human frailties and shortcomings (short**goings** too?). So maybe we **need** more princi**pled** presenters who will stick to their principal task of leading us back to basic principles!

Prominent (Mis)pronunciations

For much of my life, I think I've been guilty of emphasizing certain syllables (of certain words) that I now realize are better left **un**emphasized or **de**-emphasized. Now that I've been exposed, in various venues, to alternative emphases, I recognize my former practices as a bit tacky. We're not talking real errors here, just pronunciations that sound somewhat grating to the trained ear.

I'll mention a few examples of what I mean so you can **see** what I mean. There's "RO-mance" instead of "ro-MANCE"; "DEE-tail" instead of "de-TAIL"; "FI-nance" for "fi-NANCE"; "UM-brel-la" for "um-BREL-la"; and "REE-search" for "re-SEARCH."

In all these cases, putting the stress on the **first** syllable, which I myself habitually did, has the effect of sounding strange to refined tastes. If one simply checks the dictionary, one finds that stress belongs preferably on the **second** syllable. I'll leave it at that. They who have ears to hear the differences, let them hear!

P.S. I've also discovered that words like "electoral," "pastoral," and "mayoral" carry their emphasis on the syllable **before** the middle one (the "or" or "tor" part). Thus, the correct pronunciations are "e-LEC-tor-al," "PAS-tor-al," and "MAY-or-al." (One can look these up also, just to be sure.) We don't say "may-OR" or "pas-TOR" or "e-lec-TOR," so why should we say "may-OR-al" or "pas-TOR-al" or "e-lec-TOR-al"? Please think it over!

Proper Punctuation

Here's a helping of hot "p's porridge": When you, perhaps, prepare to provide and promote a portfolio of popular platitudes, please put your **punctuation** in **proper** places promptly!

One question that arises in this regard is: to comma or not to comma? Let's say you insert a name after the word "wife" after a man's name—e.g., "Brad's wife, Julie." A comma on one or both sides (**not** "either side") of the name "Julie" would indicate that Brad has but one wife. ("Julie" would be in apposition to "wife.") But the **omission** of a comma or commas around "Julie" would show that she is one of Brad's **multiple** wives (namely, that **particular** one). In that case, Brad would be criminally under a **cloud**—a "big-uh-**mist**"!

Now for a challenge to test your skill level. Please properly punctuate the following group of words in the same sequence so they make sense: "Bob where Bill had had had had had had had had had had had a better reception from the teacher." Impossible, you say? On the face of it, yes. But with commas, a period, and quote marks, the impossible becomes plausible: "Bob, where Bill had had '**had**,' had had '**had** had.' '**Had** had' had had a better reception from the teacher." Crazy, huh?

Boy, one can surely do a lot with painstaking punctuation perfectly positioned! (In short, observe proper punctuation marks.)

Prophecy/Prophesy

There are some very respected and respectable people who, because of their expertise in journalism, should understand how these two words differ. But that doesn't stop them from sometimes getting the words turned around. If even a **religion editor** for a national magazine has trouble distinguishing between "prophecy" and "prophesy," words that occur frequently in religious contexts, how are we laypeople supposed to tell them apart?

Let's **see**: "prophe**cy**" has a "c" in it and is pronounced "pro-phe-**see**." Since nouns usually pre**cede** verbs, and "c" precedes "s" in the alphabet, we can deduce that "prophecy" is the noun. By the same token, "prophe**sy**" (pronounced "pro-phe-**sigh**") is the verb, since "s" comes after "c." See?

So a prophet's job is to prophesy a prophecy. And if that's too hard to see, well, just give a sigh and forget about prophecies!

Reason Why/Reason Is Because

The reason **why** this item appears here **is because** so many persons fail to realize that the phrases "reason why" and "reason is because" contribute to substandard English. Both phrases contain a redundancy. Why? I'll tell you the reason—within reason.

The very word "reason" has in it all the elements covered by "why" and "because." So, reasonable persons using their reason should conclude that the word "reason" doesn't **need** add-ons that add nothing. It's strong enough to stand on its own.

Simply try an experiment. Every time you see or hear "reason **why**," mentally remove the "why" and you'll find that nothing is lost. The meaning is exactly the same. So why add "why"? How awkward it would be, for instance, to sing: "Oh, tell me **the reason** why the stars do shine"!

As for "reason is because," just listen to well-versed (or well-reasoned) speakers and you'll discover that they say, "The reason is **that** . . . ." Now, **that's** much better – no redundancy there! Besides, that wording sounds much more reasonable.

Restore Back/Refer Back/Track Back

"Tile and marble **restored back** to clean **again**," screamed an advertising circular, in off-the-chart decibels. "I can always **refer back** to what I heard on the tape," declared a lawyer who was preparing a case for trial (**not** Watergate).

When will "they" ever learn? Don't "they" realize that "re" **means** "back" or "again" (except when it means "concerning"!)? Would "they" add "back" also after "**realize**"—resulting in "realize **back**"?

I'm sure we've all heard (and maybe even "uttered back"—an "in" joke) phrases such as "reflect back," "return back," "refer back," and "restore back." That "back word" is really a step **backward** in terms of employing correct English. The "back" part is so redundant that it begs to be dropped!

In similar fashion, "track back" gets thrown around quite recklessly. For instance, a news report stated: "The police **tracked** the car **back** to its owner." (They could just as well have **traced** it back!) But think: can you track or trace something **forward**, into the **future**? Maybe it "happens" in these sci-fi movies that abound, but not in normal life. (I'm still wondering how they succeeded in going "back to the future"!)

Tracking may occur with reference to something in the present, as on a computer, but it's usually connected with an event or person in the past. So the expression "track back" is yet another redundancy.

Now that we **have** learned (as opposed to some who may never learn), we'll never **re**turn to those "re/back" combinations, will we? (Re-**ups** are okay, though!)

Sherbet/Sherbert/Sorbet

I have a confession to make. For many years, as I was growing up, I referred to a certain frozen dessert as "**sherbert**." That's the way the word was spelled and pronounced in our family, and that's the way I heard and spoke it.

How shocked I was to find out later that the word is spelled and pronounced "**sherbet**"—minus the second "r" in "sherbert"! So now, whenever I order a dish of sherbet, it's a **sure bet** that I say it the way it should be said. One good thing about mistakes is that we almost always learn from them!

Fast-forward now to my "golden years." Along comes a word that's new to me: "sorbet." I don't detect much difference in meaning or appearance from "sherbet," but how do I pronounce it? Is it "**sore**-but" (see the dangling monkey on page 13) or "sore-**bay**"? After checking two dictionaries, I'm still confused. An American dictionary lists "**sore**-but" first and "sore-**bay**" second. **But** an English dictionary (from England, that is) has the two pronunciations reversed, with "sore-**bay**" in the primary position.

I guess the upshot is that you can take your pick. If you order sherbet, you may get sorbet. And if you choose sorbet, you may receive **sherbert**, which one dictionary posits as an **alternative** to "sherbet"!

Hey, maybe my family's way of speaking back then wasn't so out-of-it, after all. All I know for sure is that we surely enjoyed our whatever-you-call-it frozen dessert!

Sit/Set

You've probably heard this old tale (whether true or legendary, I cannot **tell**): "For want of a nail, the shoe was lost; for want of a shoe, the horse was lost; and for want of a horse, the battle was lost." There's a slight parallel with a couple of common verbs, though the stakes are not as high: "For want of a proper vowel—a small letter in the middle of a small word—communication may get screwed up."

I'm referring to two of the most basic actions we humans (not "we **as** humans") carry out: **sit** and **set**. If I tell you to **sit** down, you know what to do. But if I tell you to **set** down, you may be totally unsettled! How can these simplest of terms get mixed up?

No doubt the confusion stems from the way words were spoken in our homes when we were growing up. If our parents used "set" for the act of sitting down, we tend to follow that custom, though most other people today recognize it as an error. "Sit" doesn't have or take an object. "Set" usually **does** require an object, unless we're speaking of the sun. For example, we say: "Set the table, please." (Even a "setting" hen **lays down eggs**, though she also **sits** on them.)

So if you're **set** (an adjective, not a verb) on sitting down, or "**setting yourself**" down (that's right: "setting" has an object here), to settle the difference between "sit" and "set," you may need to ask yourself if you're too **set** in your ways. (I should have warned you that this was a setup!)

P.S. Does an Irish setter sit "er" set, or **both**?

Sit or Stand Quietly/Quiet

What does it mean to sit **quietly**? I suppose it's the opposite of sitting **noisily**. But how does one sit noisily, then? Your guess is as good as mine!

It's hard to imagine varying decibels of sitting and standing. You may stand sideways, perhaps, as in a leaning position. But can you stand **loudly**, without stomping up and down? Does it take an **adverb** to describe the action of sitting or standing? Ah, that's the question—or there's the **rub**, if you happen to be rubbing against something while standing or sitting.

When we talked about "feeling" (on page 25), we said that it's ordinarily a linking verb that requires a predicate **adjective** to describe the person who's feeling a certain way. The same holds true for the verbs "sit" and "stand." They need to be followed by adjectives like "quiet" and "helpless," rather than adverbs like "quietly" and "helplessly." "Quiet" and "helpless" tellus (whoops; that should be "tell us") about the **person** rather than the kind of sitting or standing that's going on.

Now, if you're being taught how to relax or meditate, the instructor may mistakenly advise that you "spend a few minutes **sitting silently**" or that you "**lie quietly** on your bed and think happy thoughts." Having learned **different** (not "different**ly**"), you could reply, "I'd rather sit **silent** and lie **quiet**." That should put the **quietus** on the whole affair!

P.S. "Sit in silence" probably sounds more natural than "sit silent." So try sitting **in silence** while you meditate.

Slight/Sleight (of Hand)

What's the size or strength of your hand? If your hand is fairly small or weak, you could say that you are "**slight** of hand." You probably wouldn't be very handy at doing things like handicrafts. But if you had **sleight** of hand, you could work magic or trickery.

Maybe we can grasp the distinction by thinking of "Magic" Johnson, a former basketball star. He was surely **sleight** of hand (at stealing the ball and dribbling), but he probably wasn't **slight** of hand—because he needed big, strong hands to do his thing.

Hands that are quicker than the eye are capable of sleightfulness. (If that was never a word, it is now!) I don't mean to slight you, but very few persons are truly sleight of hand—a very slight minority. So you would have to work and train very hard, not slightly, to convert a **slight** hand into a **sleight** hand! (Why not try it?)

Sure/Surely

Surely you know how to tell "sure" and "surely" apart. I'm sure you know that "sure" is an adjective and "surely" an adverb. So why bother to include them on a precious page of this compact compendium?

Ah, there's many a slip twixt lip and tongue; so sometimes "sure" slips out when "surely" is surely better. "I sure do hope so" is a common saying, no matter where you happen to be. But which noun or pronoun does that adjective "sure" happen to modify in that saying? Surely not "I"! So we're left with the verb, "do hope," as the **modify-ee**, which happens to take an **adverb** modifier: "surely." I **surely do hope** that you see why "sure" is out of place here.

But we're not going to reform the world of language habits overnight. I'm under no illusion that everyone is going to get "sure" and "surely" straightened out in a hurry. Surely there's no time like the present, though, to get a reformation started. How does that song or prayer go about making the world a better place . . . beginning with **me?!**

It's a sure bet that the surest way to cure your doubts about getting a handle on the **sure** uses of "surer," "surely," and "surety" (to name a few words with "sure" within them) is to be **pure** with whatever you're sure **about**!

P.S. For the younger set, "Be Sure with Pure" was an old-time advertising slogan. Sorry to leave you wondering.

That/Which

"That which" is a common phrase, and I have nothing against it. It's even used in the Bible—e.g., "That which we have seen and heard we declare to you" (1 John 1:3). (Aside: The word "what" can be substituted for "that which" without a change in meaning.)

But many times we have to **choose** between employing "that" or "which." Then we run into a problem. We need to ask ourselves, "Which is **which**, 'that' or 'which'?" Which one we settle on is important, all of which makes for an intriguing discussion!

A publisher's stylebook makes this distinction: "Use 'that' to introduce a restrictive or essential clause. In a nonessential clause use 'which,' preceded by a comma." The **comma** is the key element to observe, whether in seeing it or in using it. A short rule would be: "That" doesn't have a comma before it, but "which" does.

Let's say you want to describe a stage play you went to. You could boast, "The play that I saw last night was terrific." In this case, "that" occurs without a comma before it. The clause it introduces is **essential** because it refers to **the** particular play you saw, not **a** different one.

But if you said, "The play *Crime and Punishment*, which I saw last night, was terrific," you would be employing a **non**essential clause introduced by "which" with a comma preceding it. The play **has already been identified** by its title, so the "which clause" simply provides additional information and serves as a filler.

Which is which? It depends on that which (or **what**) you intend to communicate. Look before you leap, **which** is good advice **that** will stand you in good stead!

There's (with Plurals)

Would you say, "There are gold in them thar hills"? Of course not. Aside from the fact that "them thar" is a trifle colloquial, "there are" just doesn't cut it when followed by a singular noun. We would consider "there are gold" totally freakish; in fact, we'd probably be freaked **out**!

So why do we completely turn the other way when so many persons follow "there's" ("there **is**") with a **plural** subject? I'm not only freaked out by this; I'm flabbergasted!

I don't have to provide examples of this common error, but I'll do it anyway. A former U. S. president once said, "I don't think **there's** many **options** left." "**There's** lots of good **things** happening," uttered a not-so-famous person, "and **there's opportunities** galore out **there**."

I suppose it's easy to slip **into** the lazy routine of combining "there's" with plurals, especially when we hear and see this slip-**up** so often. It just slips **out**, doesn't it? Maybe if we offered **gold coins** as a bribe, we could reverse the trend. But then there wouldn't be as much gold **left** in them thar hills!

Try and/Try to & Be Sure and/ Be Sure To

How often haven't you heard someone say, "I will try and do that" or "I will try and go there"? Many speakers and writers have fallen into the irritating habit of using "and" between "try" and whatever verb comes next. But think! Use some logic! "And" indicates **two** actions, separate and (supposedly) equal. First I will **try** something, and then I will **do** it.

But is that the intended sense? Most often, not. The usual **intended** sense is that I will try **to** do something—**one** action, not two. The "try" part is a helper; it's subsidiary to the main event. So can we try **to** overcome the lazy tendency to use the thoughtless "try and . . ."? Try it and see how much better "try to" sounds! (Notice the "it" between "try" and "and." That makes the construction okay. There are two distinct actions.)

The same principle holds for the phrase "Be sure and . . ."—as in "If I can help you, be sure and let me know." The intended meaning is: I want you to let me know whether I can help you. The "be sure and" part is purely extraneous. If you **do** help me, I'll surely **know** that you were sure about it. But if you (the reader) insist on inserting a "be sure," please say: "Be sure TO let me know." That's the best way, for sure!

2000 and 10/ 20-10

This item may soon be dated, but I want to get it on record anyway. It isn't an error in the strict sense of a mistake in grammar or spelling, but it is (at least in my opinion) another loophole in logic.

So often we hear the years of the "oughts" pronounced "2000 **and** 8," "2000 **and** 9," "2000 **and** 10," **and** so forth. Why all the "ands"? My goodness, we didn't find it practical to utter "1900 and 98" or "1900 and 99," did we? That would have sounded stilted or even snooty! The usual pronunciations were "19-98" or just " '99."

Let's now apply these principles to the decade of the 2000s and beyond. Instead of "2000 and 10," we could say (or could have said), "2000-10" or simply "20-10." Wow! Imagine all the "ands" omitted and therefore "saved"! What's that acronym KISS stand for? Something about keeping it simple?

"Going forward," as the "in" expression now has it (or more sensibly, in future years), can't we be content with "20-11" and "20-12," and on and on, instead of (horrors!) "2000 **and** 11," "2000 **and** 12," etc.? A breath or a word saved is a breath or a word gained. Give me 10 (or 20-10, if you have the time)!

P.S. For those who fail to realize it, the "going" in "**going** forward" is a **dangling participle**, unless followed by "I," "we," "they," or a similar word denoting **who** or **what** is "going." Please!

Unique/Uniquer

As we move toward (not "towards") the end of this thin volume, it's my hope that you will find it **unique** among the voluminous volumes out there that deal with English grammar and other linguistic issues.

I was about to write "**rather** unique," but I remembered that "unique" can't be qualified by modifiers such as "rather," "somewhat," or "very." Unique is unique is unique! It means one of a kind. An object or quality is either unique or not unique—period.

You can imagine, then, how startled I was during an important meeting to hear a professional person with high intelligence come out with the phrase "**more** unique"! Say what? How can something be more unique if it can't be **compared** with anything else? We're talking one of a kind, remember? "Unique" is an **absolute** term, though it isn't absolutely unique! (It has synonyms.)

To top things off, later in the same meeting this person coined the word "uniquer." Now, that's **really** a unique word! Supposedly, it's the comparative degree of the adjective "unique." But it certainly hurts one's ears when it's spoken. (You won't find it in a dictionary.)

P.S. Other absolute terms that shouldn't be modified or qualified are "unanimous," "perfect," "equal," and "fatal." That is almost perfectly clear, and I am just about equally unanimous in stating it, even though it's a nearly fatal flaw in my reasoning!

Unnecessary "As"-es

You've heard it times without end: that extra "as" thrown in to modify words referring to classes of people. I give you "we **as** parents," "we **as** Americans," "**as** adults, we know better," and so on, as the case may be.

Do we users of English know better than to insert so many "as"-es? I have my doubts. Isn't it better and simpler to say, "**We adults** know better"? What is gained by the superfluous "as"? It's already obvious that we're adults; otherwise, we probably **wouldn't** know better! (Let the reader understand.)

The same goes for "as parents," "as believers," and "as citizens." If we replace "as" with the word that ordinarily (unfortunately) **follows** the word that designates the class of people—namely, "we"—we end up with "we parents," "we believers," and "we citizens," followed by whatever verb applies. That sounds much smoother and more sensible!

As readers of this book, you—I mean, **you readers** of this book are aware that we as students of good English—I mean, **we students** of good English must always guard against those who, as well-meaning authors and orators—I mean, **those well-meaning authors and orators** who fail to polish their presentations and thus **de**mean our language. (I hope that long sentence is perfectly clear!)

Vice Versa/Vi-ce Versa

Are you a "vice versa" person or a "vi-suh versa" person? There **is** a difference, right? A "vice" person is **nicer** than a "vi-suh" person, even though too **many** vices isn't necessarily "ni-suh"! (Vice **versus** nice is no contest. Vice usually wins.)

Let me turn this thing around, as it were. You see, "versa" comes from the Latin word *verto*, which means "**I turn**." So when you run into anything with a "versa" in it, you will realize that a turning is involved. **You** may even have to do a **U**-turn to get where **you** want to be!

Of course, someone who **does** have too many vices will need to do a "versa" (a turnaround) in order to be nicer than a "vi-suh" person. Consequently, that would be called a "versa **vice**"—turning things around by putting the versa **before** one's vices in order to go straight. Got that?

The light at the end of the tunnel is getting a little brighter now, though we still have a few more turns in the tunnel to negotiate. (That's what you **do** with turns, isn't it? You negotiate them!)

To turn this topsy-turvy twister on its intoxicated noggin, we must **re**turn to a reliable source such as a good dictionary or a word-processing word processor. There we learn that "vice versa" is **three** syllables, not **four**. So if you're in the disconcerting habit of saying "vi-suh ver-suh," please do a 180-degree **turn** and switch to "vice ver-suh."

Pardon me if **I** turn over a new leaf now and overturn this whole contro**versy**. What was that song about four turns: "Turn, turn, turn, turn . . ."?

Vise/Vice

A word of advice to the wise will be sufficient: I would ad**vise** you not to confuse **vise** and **vice**. Some advertisements show a **vise** and call it a "vice." Now, it isn't a vice to **use** a vise, but it **is** a vice to call a vise a vice—and vice versa! (Tell me if this squeezes your brain too much, and I'll re**vise** it.)

I hope this wise advice will help you avoid similar vices. (It's okay, though, to **pay** for your vise with a **VISA®** card, which is not to be confused with vis-à-vis!)

P.S. "Vice" for "vise" is standard usage in Britain, opposite to (vis-à-vis) the spelling in the United States. But Americans have their vices as well, such as consulting too many ad**vise**rs.

Wait on/Wait For

What do you think of the interrogatory sentence "Do you spend time **waiting on** the Lord?" or the declarative sentence "We **wait on** God"? In Psalm 27:14 we read: "Wait **for** the Lord"; and again, in Psalm 130:6: "My soul **waits for** the Lord."

Isn't it better to assume that the sacred writings have word choices right and that we sometimes get them wrong? In common parlance, "waiting on" someone means **serving** that person, whether with food or some other kind of assistance. And that's the way it should be. But when we want to indicate that we're **anticipating** someone's help or arrival, we properly say that we're **waiting for** that person.

It's true that believers do serve the Lord. But does "waiting on" him in prayer or worship mean **serving** him in that situation? Not in the usual sense of the term. So we need to get our prepositions straight. We wait **for** the Lord by anticipating (yes, even praying for) the arrival of his help, help that often includes waiting **on** (serving) other people!

P.S. If you're a waiter or a waitress, you could practice greeting your customers this way: "I hope you haven't been **waiting** too long **for** me to **wait on** you."

Ways in Which

The speaker said, "We are always looking for ways in which we can keep moving." We could be charitable and assume he was using two extra words ("in which") as a stalling technique, to buy time so he could think of **ways** to complete the sentence. Or we could be **un**charitable and assume that he just didn't know better. After all, he was being redundant, whether he was aware of it or not.

That speaker was one of legions upon legions who spout "ways in which" as a matter of course. **Of course**, isn't "in which" **supposed to** follow "way" or "ways"? Not if you look hard at the way "way" conveys meaning. It shows the road or path in which one is to proceed. Ah, there! "In which" is **already present** within "way." People today would say it's **embedded** in its predecessor.

So why add an add-on that adds nothing and is completely unnecessary? Every time you see or hear "way(s) in which," simply take out "in which" and you'll discover that the meaning hasn't changed an iota. For example, "the way we wash our clothes" is simpler and shorter than "the way in which we wash our clothes."

Now we have another **way** to "tighten." If one of your **ways** (habits) is to say things like "ways in which to keep moving," start dropping "in which" and keep moving. Way to go!

P.S. It's okay to use "in which" after the word "manner," a synonym of "way." What other way is there?

Whence/Thence

These two words may be unfamiliar to modern audiences, especially younger persons. "Whence" and "thence" belong to a previous era when formal language prevailed. But once in a while we may run across these expressions, so it helps to be acquainted with them. Hence their inclusion here.

Suppose someone asks you "from **whence**" you have come. Instead of giving a blank stare, you could reply: "I guess you want to know **where** I've come from." That would show that you know "whence" means "from where." The problem is, "**from** whence" is redundant. It's like saying, "**From** from where have you come?"

The same holds true for the expression "from **thence**." Since "thence" means "from **there**," you can see why the "from" in "from thence" is unnecessary and pointless. (If the formal "from thence" continues to be preferred in a creedal statement, at least the word "from" could be omitted. But "from there" would be much clearer.)

Hence, the "whences" and "thences" are **henceforth** better left to stand on their own, minus the "froms"—if this makes sense without being dense or leaving you tense!

Whether/Whether or Not

I don't know whether to tango with the tangled "knot" of "whether or not," because it may be hard to **un**tangle. But whether it's too difficult or not, I guess I'll weather the possible storm of dissent!

I just used both "whether" and "whether or not" in the same paragraph, I trust you **ga**thered. "Whether" is **ra**ther temperamental; sometimes it wants "not" along, and sometimes **not**. So how do we decide?

Maybe the best way is to remove "or not" from "whether or not" and see **whether** this omission makes any difference in meaning. For instance, a student may sigh aloud, "I don't know whether or not I'll pass this test." If we take out "or not," the statement still makes sense—not? In fact, "or not" is **redundant**, because it's already **built into** "whether"! That's what "whether" means here: either this or **that**; I'll either pass the test or I won't.

Though many persons automatically mouth "whether or not" **all the time**, whether it's fitting or not, most of the time we're better off **without** "or not." But if a sentence doesn't make **sense** without "or not," leave it in. (See the first sentence in this paragraph.)

Whether you agree with all this **or not**, I hope the **weather** where you are is delightful!

Which/This

Is "which" a proper word with which to begin a sentence? If the sentence is a question (e.g., "Which way are you going?"), or a sentence beginning with a "which" modifier (e.g., "Which way you go is important"), fine. But I would contend that "which" is misused if it stands alone as a summary of what has gone before (e.g., "**Which** makes it certain that all is not well").

Who gave people—even prominent, well-educated people—license to substitute "which" for "this"? After all, one of the purposes of "this" is to serve as a bridge or transition between what has gone before and what comes after. So the sentence at the close of the previous paragraph would preferably read: "**This** makes it certain that all is not well."

Which is—I'm sorry; **This** is—to say that "which" is often out of place at the start of a sentence. So switch some of your "whiches" to "thises," lest you become "be-**whiched**," bothered, and bewildered. (Forgive me for getting carried away by such "**which**-craft"!)

Who/That

Quote: "A president that launches policies he can't sustain isn't doing his job." Do you agree or disagree with that? You may agree with the accusation, but what about the word choices? Take another look at the third word in that opening quotation—namely, "that." Of course, "that" is much better than a word like "which," because it defines and limits the kind of president being discussed. But **that** isn't the point.

The point is that "**that**" is the wrong word! People aren't "thats"! Thats are **things** (or animals, unless named). People of any stripe are logically followed by the relative pronoun "who." Wouldn't you rather be called a **who** than a **that**, an impersonal thing? I thought so. Remember the elephant Horton, who proclaimed: "A Who is a Who, no matter how small"? So "who" trumps "that" in a relative clause after a named person or personal title.

Someone once asked, "Which word does one use after the word 'family'—'who' or 'that'?" Well, is "family" a person? Not exactly. A family is a group of persons, an entity. So we properly say, "The family **that** prays together stays together," not "The family **who** pray together stay together." Got **that**? That's a quick learner, **who**ever you are!

Who/Whom

To get "who" and "whom" straightened out is pretty much an uphill battle. The use of "who" in both subjective and objective cases is nearly universal, at least in predominantly English-speaking countries. We hear "Who likes you?" and "Who do you like?" in almost the same breath. Has "**whom**" been banished to another **galaxy**? It seems so, unfortunately.

A pastor's sermon included this bit of wisdom: "The important thing is not **how** we worship but **who** we worship." Of course the "who" is important, but so is the grammar! No doubt God was listening and was able to forgive, or at least wink an eye at, this departure from standard English. But maybe, just maybe, some other listeners were distracted enough to miss out on the pearls of wisdom in the **next** part of the sermon.

It **may be** too much to expect that we can put the genie (with the light-brown hair?) back in the bottle and restore the proper use of "whom" in spoken communication. But in **visual** communication, on paper or online or in texting, the sender has time and opportunity to review the message and add an "m" after "who" in case the objective case is in order.

For example, wouldn't it be perplexing to come across "To WHO it may concern" in place of "To WHOM it may concern"? I think so too-hoo! Don't you-hoo?

Wordiness

We have already propounded the principle of "tightening" (see page 41). But since the profusion of excess verbosity and verbiage (a deliberate redundancy on my part) is so widespread, it isn't exces**sive** to consider this topic once more. An oft-repeated maxim in the area of learning is "Repetition is the mother of studies." (I hear these words often in dreams of my father.)

We will not here discuss the language of the legal profession. We recognize that legal terminology in contracts, wills, and warranties has to be precise and extensive so as to ward off any ambiguity or challenge. However, the communications of public companies and institutions are fair game, because their goal is to be clear, brief, and easily understood by everyone. The pronouncements even (and especially) by high officials in government and commerce are considered "doublespeak" if they are drawn out and convoluted.

To shorten this already lengthy essay, I'll quote two examples of **wordiness** and then translate the foggy messages into "**single**speak," so to speak:

"As always, however we can be of assistance to you, please don't hesitate to be in contact with us." **Translation**: "If we can help you, please tell us." (19 words transposed into 8.)

"**As a valued customer** of our bank, **we** (!!) wanted to take this opportunity to let you know of two great products." **Translation**: "Here are two great products for you." (21 words into 7.)

P.S. I can't help wondering why we're constantly reminded "not to hesitate" or to "feel free" to contact the message senders. **Hesitation** hardly enters the mind of someone seeking assistance, and who feels **enslaved** to ask for help?!

Wreaking Havoc
(WRECKing or REEKing?)

(This will be a "shortie," for a change. It's an error only in pronunciation.)

Some persons in very high places have been heard to pronounce these two words as "**wrecking** havoc." Well, that's quite a wreck to impose on the word "**wreaking**," which means "causing." (Notice that there's an "a" in the center of the word, not a "c.")

A quick look at a dictionary settles the issue: The proper pronunciation of "wreaking" is REEKing, even if this makes it smell to high heaven! So when we're about to cause havoc in some manner, let's "reek" it, not "wreck" it—although the wreaking of **damage** may **leave** a wreck!

You Know/I Mean/Whatever

Every time I hear someone say, "I mean, you know, . . . ," I'm tempted to reply, "No, I **don't** know what you **mean**!" But that would be disrespectful, you know.

Do **you** know why people use "you know" so much? I think I know. It's because **they** don't know the next word or words to supply. They're trying to think of what next to say, or they're searching for the right thing to say, so they **fill in** with "you know." It's a delaying tactic, a gap-filler, until the next phrase comes to mind.

I mean, you know as well as I know that "you know" is a bit icky. But adding it whenever and wherever we feel like it is an "**add**-iction" that's hard to break. If we want to overcome this irksome habit, we need to fight it. Maybe we ought to get counseling! Or perhaps we could join a "you-know anonymous" group! (We could call it "Euonymus.") Whatever!

Now, don't get me started on the overuse of, you know, I mean, "**whatever**"! (Whatever made me think of **that**? I really mean, I don't **know**.)

Afterword

This "top 100" set is just a sample of the errors rampant out there. More books on this topic could be prepared, I'm sure. But somehow we manage to survive and make our way through life. Most people get things mostly right most of the time. Otherwise, we wouldn't be able to function in society. Of course, regional dialects exist, so what's unacceptable or frowned on in many places may be perfectly understood and accepted in other places. Hard-and-fast rules sometimes have to be softened and slowed to allow for local customs.

*This whole exercise in considering common errors is about fine-tuning. (Everybody **wants** to be fine, right?) If you picked up only half a dozen or so new ideas, the process has been worth it. You can enjoy sharing your fresh insights with friends at coffee breaks or in the school cafeteria, if you're modest and tactful about it.*

Other people often judge us by the way we speak and write, and vice versa. A person who uses correct language is admired, trusted, and perhaps even **rewarded** (if that person is asking for a favor or a donation). Moreover, a grasp of proper English helps us "screen" phone callers who want to sell us something, letter writers or Internet advertisers who try to persuade us in some fashion, and speakers who play on our emotions. We can say to ourselves, "I know things about language that convince me they don't understand how to express themselves correctly. So I don't have to yield to their pitches or be persuaded by their illogical reasoning. Often I can simply tune them out."

*Indeed, it **does pay** to be "in the know." As a welcome bonus, your friends and relatives will be glad they know **you!***

A Supplement for Students

Sometimes you may hear a comment like "Oh, that's a book you'll never use." Some books **do** find little use and end up with their dust jackets covered with dust. But the savvy you've gained in the foregoing pages **will** prove useful in the future. Even right now you may find this guidebook helpful if you're in a creative writing class. And remember, the good examples we set **throughout** our lives have far-reaching benefits in the hearts and minds of those who come after us.

*A secret tip: Putting into practice the improvements noted in this book could raise your language-arts grade a notch or two—but only if you actually absorb them. To accomplish this, you may need to review some articles several times and let them soak in. But the adventure promises to be fun, not boring. In fact, you may wind up knowing more in certain key areas than columnists and editors in leading magazines! Many errors referred to herein were culled directly from their published work. (I recently found three dangling participles on one page. Imagine! Example: "Growing up, **his family** owned a bar." And the editors let it pass.)*

A playful suggestion is that you rate which entries appealed to you the most. Grade the items with A-B-C's or use asterisks so you can return to your favorites and concentrate on them. Not everyone will like the same ones, but most persons will probably have some preferences. Make them your own, whether they be 5 or 25!

And if you want to really excel in English, study the Latin language, which is the basis for five other languages: Spanish, French, Portuguese, Italian, and Romanian. In many ways Latin also helps us understand English better, not the least of which is word derivation. If you know the meaning of a Latin root or stem, it's far easier to grasp the English word(s) based thereon.

A semifinal word: If you want to get your face out of this book, you may go to Facebook and look for me there. But I won't promise to meet you face to face. I'll just do an about-face and have a face-off!

P.S. For younger students who are reading this book, or who have read it already, be advised that in some instances there are different levels of meaning. That's because a lot of words have several meanings, and the differences may not be readily apparent. For example, you may need to look up all the meanings of "altogether" in order to understand every way it is used on a certain page. But if you don't catch every nuance (and that's okay), try again in a few years, after you've had more life experiences. Then, suddenly, things may be clearer to you. Is that a deal? I hope so! *Kam sa ham nee dá* (Korean expression for "thank you").

Appendix 1

An appendix tends to just hang on. The following "hangers-on" are shorter items that didn't require a separate page in the body of the book. The number of "extras" in this potpourri could have run into the hundreds, but space and time did not allow. The ones included here are those that came to mind during the book's conception, inception, and completion.

Please note that in the section on mispronunciations, some divergence in opinion is to be expected. Dictionaries often present more than one possible sound; however, the first one given is preferred in general usage, so that principle has been followed. You may not always agree with what is written, but the right to write it is rightfully the author's.

We do learn from one another; else we would continue in our erroneous ways. For example, I once thought that "café" was one syllable: "CAFE"! I also had to learn that "mediocre" wasn't pronounced "medicore" (that was before the days of Medicare). So if through these listings you receive some new insights, welcome to the club!

Common Misspellings

Accidentally is still the right spelling, though "accidently" may show up in a word-search engine. Dropping the letters "al" is simply a convenient corruption.

Afterward, backward, downward, forward, inward, outward, toward, and **upward** are preferred in American English over the corresponding forms with an added "s" (e.g., "afterwards," "towards," etc.). British English favors the additional "s." But why employ an extra letter? The simpler, the better is a good rule to follow (exception: "innards"!).

All right is definitely all right, as opposed to "alright," which has never been accepted as a standard variant. In this rare case, two words are actually better than one!

Daylight-saving time is correct. "Daylight-savings time" is incorrect. This customary changeover isn't the same as a **savings** account!

Descendant refers to someone whose descent can be traced to another person. "**Descendent**" (with an "e" as the third-last letter) means "moving downward"; it's an adjective, not a noun. Trust me!

Forebears is sometimes misspelled and mispronounced as "forebearers." The word refers to one's ancestors, none of whom are **bears**! (And there are doubtless more than four.)

Grievous and **mischievous** do not have an extra "i" or an extra syllable after the "v." Avoid "grievious" and "mischievious," if it doesn't grieve you or lead to mischief.

Judgment rendered by a judge does not become a "judgement." Whether a judge likes it or not, the "e" is lost when "judge" is joined to "ment." I guess it was **meant** to be, in my judgment.

Lightning bolts and bugs don't like an "e" in the center of their names. Forget "lightening," unless a load is being lightened.

More important is better than "more importantly." Why? "More important" includes an implied "what is" before it. Thus, "important" is an adjective modifying "what." (This item could also go under "Wrong Words Used.")

Revelation is the name of the Bible's last book, not "Revelations." That may be a revelation to some persons, but so be it!

Supersede supersedes the incorrect "supercede." I hope you'll cede me that!

Worldview has replaced "world view" and "world-view," some reputable writers and editors notwithstanding. The word is a direct translation of the German *Weltanschauung*, a single word.

Worshiped and **worshiping** have evolved in the U.S. from "worshipped" and "worshipping," though the change unfortunately hasn't caught on in a few places.

More Redundancies

A new innovation is indeed news to me! Has anyone ever come up with an **old** innovation? "Innovate" comes from the Latin root word *novus*, which **means** "new." So we don't need a **new** new thing.

Additional funding was also provided is overdoing the funding. "Also" adds insult to injury, so to speak—another word we can do without.

But nevertheless covers the same ground twice. How long will we suffer two adversatives hand-running? Would anyone say "but however"? But that's another issue, however!

Each one is a bit over the top. Unless a strong emphasis is desired, "each" is sufficient. It **means** "one of two or more," so why add another "one"?

Have got to has over 50 years of entrenching itself in the American psyche. But have we considered what role the "got" plays? It isn't only unnecessary; it's also poor English. **Have** you **got** that?

Once again I beg you to consider the need for that "once." Does its presence mean the speaker or writer is going to continue with "twice again" and "thrice again"? Again is again is again, in my book. (This **is** my book!)

Over and above sounds a little like stuttering. What's the difference between "over" and "above"? If you're driving over the speed limit, you're also going above it. Do you want to pay **two** fines? (Members of the legal profession, please coddle me if this expression is a legal term, as it may well be. **For you**, I'll make an exception.)

Throughout the entire needlessly spends an extra word. "Throughout the system" means entirely the same as "throughout the **entire** system," because "throughout" means all through the whole thing! Is that entirely clear throughout?

Today and every day is one day too many. "Today" is **one of** the "every days." Therefore, if we insist on including it, we must separate it from the rest by saying "today and **all other** days." (But "tomorrow is **another** day"!)

Where it's at contains a superfluous word: "at." Just stop with "where it **is**." "At" is **built into** the concept of "where." If you ever hear "82 degrees is where the mercury will top out at," you may want to apply for the job of weather forecaster. A replacement is sorely needed!

Wrong Words Used

A free gift could be classified as a redundancy, but it's included here because a better choice of phrase is in order. "An undeserved gift" is more appropriate, as is "an unrestricted gift" or "a boundless gift." But as we know, the gift without the giver is bare. (I hope that isn't a non sequitur.)

A while and **awhile** are both correct, but sometimes they're used incorrectly. In a prepositional phrase, "while" is a noun that serves as the object of the preposition, and it needs to be separated from the adjective "a." But as an **adverb**, "awhile" is a single word denoting length of time. So we properly use either "stay for **a while**" or "stay **awhile**." Any questions, comments, or (unwise) objections?

"Advanced" medical directives are all the rage, but the first word is an **out**rage. Haven't we advanced far enough that we know the difference between "advanced" and "advance"? For instance, a living will is a document we prepare **in advance** of when we may need it. An **advanced** directive would be one that goes beyond a previous one, but I doubt whether many of those exist. So that extra "d" is a liability!

Aren't I? is a faddish expression that supposedly conveys an element of sophistication. But when we analyze it, we find that the singular pronoun "I" is joined with a plural verb, "are." This results in "**Are I not?**" One may as well ask, "Ain't I?" The only logical way to ask the question is "**Am** I not?" Am I not right?

Entitle used to be the normal verb for "give a title to." But then someone noticed that the verb "title" means the same thing. Over time, the "en" came to be dropped by thoroughly modern communicators. So if you want to be thoroughly modern (and especially if your name is **Millie**), you're entitled to shorten the word "entitle(d)" to "title" or "titled." Now we've "saved" another two letters!

Exult, which means "be jubilant," isn't that common a word. It occurs primarily in worship settings, such as in readings from the Bible. But when we hear someone proclaim that God **exalts** over us, we have to sit up and take notice. That's a fairly exalted thing to say, but one vowel is inaccurate. The "a" should be a "u," so that we have "exults." Since a person who is exalted is usually brought low, it's better to be **exulted** over than **exalted** over.

First-come, first-serve sounds wacky because it **is** wacky. The one who arrives first is supposed to serve first? Get real! The one who comes first is supposed to be the first one **served**. So let's always go with "first-come, first-served," especially if we're the first to come!

Growing is a standard verb in the context of raising flowers and food crops. But it has become commonplace also in many other settings. We supposedly "grow" our money and our waistlines. I've seen even the phrase "growing **people** in knowledge." But I don't believe "growing" was meant to cover so much territory. Doesn't "growing people" sound weird? I much prefer "helping people grow." That use of "grow(ing)" grows on me!

Irregardless starts off with two expendable letters: "ir." The simpler "**regardless**" covers the ground intended by "without regard to." Some confusion may arise because of the similarity between "irregardless" and the legitimate word "irrespective," which means "heedless." We need to keep our ears tuned to the right "ir's"!

Loan is ordinarily a noun, not a verb. We should **lend** money, not loan it—although we can take out a loan consisting of money. (Would money lent during Lent be twice-lent?) It would sound strange to loan someone an ear, but "lending an ear" was a kosher expression in Shakespeare's day!

Plan out sounds like a fairly logical thing to say. If we plan something and it turns out well, doesn't it "plan out"? Not quite. The right idiom to use is "**pan** out." If you're panning for gold and you strike it rich, you really do pan out! "Pan out" means to be successful; it's from *patina*, a Latin word for shallow pan. If all this is too hard to remember, just stick with the phrase "work out." Then all will be perfectly clear and will work out!

Planning on doing something isn't exactly an embarrassing word choice. But planning **to** do a thing seems the better way to go. A plan is a projected design; it's something we **make**, in our heads or on paper, that we want **to** carry out. "**Depending** on" or "**counting** on" would preferably carry the sense of "planning **on**." (This may be an instance of splitting hairs, but at least I hope it isn't a **hare**brained distinction. See "harebrained" in the next section.)

Rare back is a term usually associated with baseball announcers who try to describe a pitcher's stance before the ball is thrown. But "rare" isn't even a verb! So it would be a rare sight indeed to see a pitcher (or even a horse) "rare back"! If we change "rare" to "rear," we're in business and we may win the game. "Rearing back" is in good form, even though the form of a pitcher's back isn't always in the rear during a windup.

Track rack is hard to justify as a device for holding **tracts**. But at times the awkward term does creep in (unintentionally, I trust). It's much better to keep "track" of tracts by placing them where they belong: in a **tract rack!**

Two or More Words Confused

Biennial sounds almost like "**biannual**." But there's quite a difference between the two descriptives—about a year and a half's worth. If meetings occur biennially, they happen once every two years. But **biannual** meetings take place twice each year. Be sure to check your schedule before you pack your bags. You may miss out on a biannual event if you think it's a **biennial** one!

Competence, hesitance, relevance, equivalence, and **resilience** belong to a family of nouns that prefer the ending "ce" over the ending "cy." Ours is not to know why, but simply to obey. When we come to "**redundancy**," though, we find that "cy" takes precedence (or should that be "precedency"?). **See** what I mean when I confess that sometimes there's no rhyme or reason in the development of language? Our **hesitance** to learn and practice the finer points may lead to the cropping up of **redundancies**. But we wouldn't want to be known as "duncies," would we?

Disassociate means "to remove from association." "**Dissociate**" also means "to remove from association." With which verb do you wish to be associated? Remember the KISS acronym? That's usually the more desirable approach. (It can even be caressing!)

Hairbrained, sorry to say, is not a word. If it were, it wouldn't be a compliment, because it would mean "with a hair-size brain." "**Harebrained**" **is** a word; it means "with no more sense than a hare," which isn't much. Now, "**splitting** hares" would be a rather hairy way to double the amount of sense in hares, so we'd better leave well enough alone. Hares double fast enough as it is!

Inflammable or **flammable**—which is it? Lest you be confused, their meanings are identical. But the prefix "in" has misled some persons into thinking that "inflammable" means "**not** flammable," which isn't true. So to avoid ambiguity, we're advised to stay with "**flammable**"—unless we want to convey the idea of "easily aroused to strong emotion" (inflammable). Hey, whether we're dodging hot flames or hot anger, it's best to hightail it out of there!

It's and **its** are confused when an apostrophe is carelessly inserted in the possessive form "its." Since "it's" means **it is**, it can't take the place of "its" without looking silly. We don't write "their's," do we? (I hope not.)

Orient and **orientate** are two halves of the same coin, identical in meaning. But I wouldn't advise flipping a coin to determine which word to use. The extra "ate" at the end of the second verb is totally unnecessary, unless you desire to extend the verb to form the noun "orientation." In that case, your **inclination** would have a **tendency** to **orient** itself in the **direction** of the longer term! (Let the reader understand.)

Pouring and **poring** are separated only by an extra "u"—but what a difference that "u" makes! Quote: "Many investors start the year by **pouring** over economic forecasts." Pouring over a **rainy** forecast may get you drenched, so I'd advise you to **pore** (read carefully) over forecasts of all kinds, even if the old man **is** snoring.

Preventive and **preventative** conform to the pattern of similar words with one of them having an additional syllable. By now it should be clear that the extra syllable is just that: extraneous and unneeded. **Preventive** medicine is sufficient to help prevent diseases, without the "ta" insertion. Ta-ta-ta!

Primer and **primer** are spelled the same, but they're pronounced differently and have different meanings. A "primer" with a **short** "i" (as in "prim") is a book or another medium that presents the basic elements of a subject, such as learning to read. A "primer" with a **long** "i" (as in "prime") usually refers to an undercoat that prepares a surface for painting. I suppose if you are a painter who's learning to read, you could be studying a primer while applying a primer!

Raising cane may produce a sweet effect (if the cane is sugar), or it may bamboozle you (if the cane is bamboo). But if you're raising **Cain** (with a capital "c"), you're in a heap of trouble. Behaving in a rowdy way could lead to a Caine mutiny on the part of your friends. So it's better to stick with raising cane (**not** a walking cane or a crop of 'caine), if you're **able**!

Reoccur may have been used in times past to mean "happen again or repeatedly." But modern dictionaries, at least in the United States, don't even contain the word. Evidently, it morphed into the simpler term "**recur**," which has the same meaning. It occurs to me that the triumph of "recur" over "reoccur" is an occurrence of exceptionally good judgment!

Soft-pedal and "**soft-peddle**" [*sic*] sound alike but have entirely different meanings. To "soft-pedal" is to soften the tone of a piano or organ by depressing the soft pedal. It also means to play down in importance or go easy. To "**peddle**" is to sell; so if "soft-peddle" were an actual word, it would mean to use a soft sell. But a peddler who wants to make a sale wouldn't employ a **soft** pedal. He would try to "**hard**-pedal" his wares in order to soften a customer's resistance. Could he then be called a "hard-peddler"? You decide!

Mispronunciations
(with corrections and actual words following)

Ad'ult: **uhdult'** (adult)
Air: **uhr** (err)
Allees: **alleyes** (allies)
Anteye- & multeye-: **antee-** & **multee-** (anti- & multi-)
Archetype: **arketype** (archetype)
Artic & Antartic: **Arctic** & **Antarctic** (Arctic & Antarctic)
Ballm, callm, pallm, psallm: **bahm, cahm, pahm, psahm** (balm, calm, palm, psalm)
　　　[Look these up if you doubt. The "l" is **silent**! But beware of "bahm in Gilead."]
Bap'tize: **baptize'** (baptize)
Cantilever: **cantileever** (cantilever)
　　　[This is just the opposite of "lever"!]
Chaldea: **Kaldea** (Chaldea)
Con'summate: **consum'mate** (consummate, the adjective)
Creeaayytivity: **creuhtivity** (creativity)
Deb'uhcle: **debah'cle** (debacle)
Divissive: **diveyesive** (divisive)
Drownded: **drowned** (drowned, **one** syllable)
Eggzavier: **Zavier** (Xavier)
Ehruh: **eeruh** (era)

Ek cetera: **et cetera** (et cetera)

En rowt & en mass: **ahn root** & **ahn mahss** (en route & en masse)

Ep'itome: **epit'uhmee** (epitome)

Eyedee'ologue: **idd'eeologue** (ideologue)

Febuary: **Feb*r*uary** (February)
    [Wouldn't it be more honorable to change the spelling than to keep
    mispronouncing the word?]

Gahrentee: **gehrentee** (guarantee)

Geeneeology: **geenee*a*logy** (genealogy)

Gore-may & pore & tore-ist: **goormay** & **poohr** & **toorist** (gourmet &
    pour & tourist) [Pores are on the skin!]

Harbinger: **harbin*j*er** (harbinger)

Hosteyeuhl & mobeyeuhl & volateyeuhl: **hostul** & **mobul** & **volatul**
    (hostile & mobile & volatile)
    [But go with **texteyeuhl** (textile), an exception.]

Hy'perbowl: **hyper'bolee** (hyperbole)

Inhairent: **inheerent** (inherent)
    [It doesn't have the same root as "in**her**it."]

In'surance: **insur'ance** (insurance)

Jewlery: **jewelry** (jewelry)
    ["Jewellery" is British English.]

Leeay'zon: **lee'uhzon** (liaison)

Leever: **lever** (lever)

Madjeye: **Mayjeye** (Magi)

Magna Charta: **Magna Karta** (Magna Carta)

Momento: **m*e*mento** (memento)

Mores: **mor'ayse** (mores, **two** syllables)

Moscaccioli: **mos*t*accioli** (mostaccioli)
    [Remember that it's the **most**!]

Naive-uhté: **naive-té** (naiveté, **three** syllables)

Offten: **offen** (often)
    ["Offten" is British English.]

Omage: **homage** (homage)

Otto: **oughto** (auto)
    [Otto is a man's name.]

Pee'laf: **pilahf'** (pilaf)

Peeoh'nee: **pee'uhnee** (peony)

Pitcher: **pic-ture** (picture)

Poignant: **poi*n*yant** (poignant)

Pahtable: **pohtable** (potable)

Proboskis: **probosis** (proboscis)

Prohductivity: **prahductivity** (productivity)

Reconize: **recognize** (recognize)

Relator: **Realtor®** (Realtor®)

Repreyes: **represe** (reprise)

        [It doesn't rhyme with "surprise"!]

Set-tle-er & star-tle-ing & sti-ful-ing & dou-ble-ing: **set-tler** & **star-tling** & **sti-fling** & **dou-bling** (settler & startling & stifling & doubling—all **two** syllables)

Skizem: **sizem** (schism)

Sohlace: **sahlace** (solace)

Strenth: **strength** (strength)

Sujjest: **suggest** (suggest)

Thhee'ayter: **thhee'uhter** (theater)

Tore-us: **Tawrus** (Taurus)

        ["Au" equals "aw," **not** "or."]

Tour de force: **tour de fawrce** (tour de force)

Tours: **Tour** (Tours, a French city)

Trespassses: **trespuhses** (trespasses)

        [Practice saying "TRES-puh-ses." It's the preferred pronunciation, and it sounds much more pleasing!]

Trīst: **trĭst** (tryst)

Vaayy'cay'tion: **vuhca'tion** (vacation, only **one** syllable stressed)

Vee-hic-cle: **vee-uh-cle**, please (vehicle)

Veeuh: **veyeuh** (via)

Warshington: **Washington** (Washington)

Special Cases

As often as possible and **deepest possible**: Such expressions are a bit exaggerated. "As often as **possible**" could stretch indefinitely! "With the **deepest possible** love and concern" could deepen into a bottomless pit! Let's be content with the more realistic "as often as you're able" and "with deepest love and concern." Is **that** possible?

    Between you and I is a special case because the case of the second pronoun is wrong. The object of a preposition naturally goes in the **objective** case. (This is just between you and **me**!)

Fiancé and **fiancée** are fairly-well fixed in our minds: one final "e" for males; two "e's" for females. But there's a corresponding practice in the words "**protégé**" and "**protégée**": one final "e" for males; two for females. We can be glad that French is consistent. Would that we all were! (I will neglect "negligée.")

Illogical progressions can strain one's credence. What's wrong with this sentence: "Attend classes in Ohio, Indiana, Kentucky, or study online"? The word "or" is missing between "Indiana" and "Kentucky." "Or study online" doesn't follow logically as an equal element with the names of the states. Therefore, we have to **complete** the state names with an "or" before continuing with a separate thought: "or study online." So far the lesson in logic, which comes as a bonus with this book about errors!

Is is commonly spelled with a lower-case "i" in titles and headings. People may think it's such a short word that it doesn't deserve a capital letter. But it's the all-important VERB, so award it a big "I."

Neglected commas between or among adjectives in sequence can result in strained (or strange?) vision. Not even a dog would type: "It was a dark stormy night." The dog would add either a comma or a conjunction between the adjectives—"It was a dark, stormy night" or "It was a dark and stormy night." Commas serve to break up sequences of adjectives that modify nouns so they can be more easily absorbed. Ah, how much dogs can teach us!

Ofttimes and **oftentimes** contain an unnecessary syllable: "times." "Oft" and "often" already tell us what we need to know. The Oxford English Dictionary even calls "ofttimes" and "oftentimes" archaic. How **often** we get carried away by flowery-sounding language, even if it's dated or old-fashioned!

On behalf of myself is usually couched in a longer expression: "On behalf of (so and so) and myself." But here again, "myself" is used as a **personal pronoun**, not a reflexive or intensive pronoun (as it should be). Since "on behalf of **me**" would sound awkward, to say the least, we can easily transform the whole phrase into the much more pleasing "on **my own** behalf." Now we're talking sense!

Two sentences or two clauses without a linking conjunction often get separated with a measly comma. (Compound sentences **with** a conjunction occur even more frequently with no comma **at all**!) We have a more helpful procedure—use at least a semicolon, if not a dash or period, between the two parts. Consider these rather **ill**-considered examples: (1) "Don't just think compliments, say them." (2) "Not only do we know the names, we know the persons." Commas in themselves don't provide enough pause; therefore, **increase** the pause with a semicolon, dash, or period. (For the uninitiated, a semicolon is what you have left if part of your colon is removed!)

End of Appendix 1. Period.
(No appendectomy, however.)

Appendix 2

Since this little tome is billed as "lighthearted," it's fitting that we conclude on a humorous note. I've selected several amusing anecdotes to leave a sweet-as-sugar taste in your mouth. (Remember what a spoonful of sugar does?) The jokes have been gleaned from true accounts, though some details have been modified to protect the innocent.

The audience at an outdoor concert was asked to stand and sing along during the final musical selection. However, the printed program must have run short of ink, since the abbreviated instruction went: "Let us rise and **sin**"!

A university professor was grading reports by his students when he came across this remarkable comment: "I don't care to go up in front during church services, because I don't like the smell of the **incest**"!

A well-known author and editor was attending his mother on her deathbed. As she labored to breathe, he bent close and whispered, "Do you have any last words for my children, your dear grandchildren?" She thought for a moment and then said in a strong voice, "Tell them to shut up!"

With that, **I** will now shut up. Olé! What I have written, I have written. And the moving hand, having written, moves on . . .